ADOPTION

Blessings & Prayers —

"You have received
a Spirit of
adoption..."

Rom 8:15

[signature]

ADOPTION
Room for One More?

Jaymie Stuart Wolfe

Pauline
BOOKS & MEDIA
Boston

Library of Congress Cataloging-in-Publication Data

Wolfe, Jaymie Stuart.
  Adoption : room for one more? / Jaymie Stuart Wolfe.
    pages cm. -- (Call to adoption)
  ISBN 978-0-8198-0837-0 (pbk.) -- ISBN 0-8198-0837-7 (pbk.)
  1. Adoption--Psychological aspects. 2. Wolfe, Jaymie Stuart--Family. 3. Wolfe
family. 4. Adoptive parents--United States--Biography. 5. Intercountry adoption-
-United States. 6. Intercountry adoption--Russia (Federation) 7. Love, Maternal--
Religious aspects--Christianity. I. Title.
  HV875.5.W648 2015
  248.8'45--dc23
                        2014046057

Excerpts from the *New American Bible,* copyright © 1991, 1986, and 1970 by the Confraternity of Christian Doctrine, Washington, DC and are used by permission of the copyright owner. All rights reserved.

Excerpts from the *Book of Blessings*, additional blessings for use in the United States of America © 1988 United States Conference of Catholic Bishops, Washington, DC. All rights reserved.

All other Scripture quotations contained herein are from the *New Revised Standard Version Bible: Catholic Edition,* copyright © 1989, 1993, Division of Christian Education of the National Council of the Churches of Christ in the United States of America. Used by permission. All rights reserved.

Cover design by Rosana Usselmann

Cover photo istockphoto/com / © syntika, © NREY

"P" and PAULINE are registered trademarks of the Daughters of St. Paul.

Published by Pauline Books & Media, 50 Saint Pauls Avenue, Boston, MA 02130-3491

Printed in the U.S.A.

www.pauline.org

Pauline Books & Media is the publishing house of the Daughters of St. Paul, an international congregation of women religious serving the Church with the communications media.

1 2 3 4 5 6 7 8 9   19 18 17 16 15

For all who dare to set sail
on love's uncharted oceans,
and to the Holy Spirit
who guides them.

Contents

Introduction *1*

WHY ADOPT?

Chapter 1
Called to Be Family: *Choosing Love* 7

Chapter 2
Moved By Gratitude: *Love Turns Outward* *12*

Chapter 3
Infertility: *Love Gives Life* *17*

WHO SHOULD ADOPT?

Chapter 4
The Opinion Poll: *Love Encourages* *25*

Chapter 5

Not For Everyone: *Love Listens* *30*

Chapter 6

Special Challenges: *Love Discerns* *35*

CHOICES

Chapter 7

Pink or Blue? *Love Affirms* *43*

Chapter 8

How Old Are You? *Love Believes* *48*

Chapter 9

Cross-Racial and Cross-Cultural Adoption: *Love Stretches* *53*

Chapter 10

Special Needs Adoption: *Love Lifts* *58*

Chapter 11

Adopting More Than One Child? *Love Multiplies* *63*

THE PROCESS

Chapter 12

Domestic and International Adoption: *Love Seeks* *71*

Chapter 13

The "Right" Agency: *Love Advocates* *76*

Chapter 14

Homestudy, Medicals, and Financials: *Love Approves* 81

Chapter 15

Open or Closed Adoption? *Love Respects* 86

Chapter 16

The Paper Pregnancy: *Love Labors* 91

Chapter 17

The Waiting Parent: *Love Is Patient* 96

Chapter 18

Lost Referrals: *Love Is Vulnerable* 101

Chapter 19

Getting the Call: *Love Rejoices* 106

Chapter 20

A Day in Court: *Love Seals* 111

YOUR CHILD

Chapter 21

Meeting Your Child: *Love Knows* 119

Chapter 22

Medical Mysteries: *Love Trusts* 124

Chapter 23

The Burden of History: *Love Bears All Things* 129

Chapter 24

Birth and Adoptive Mothers: *Love Reconciles* *134*

Chapter 25

Identity and Name: *Love Recognizes* *139*

Chapter 26

The Waiting Child: *Love Hopes* *144*

HOME TOGETHER

Chapter 27

A Brand New Shiny Life: *Love Makes Everything New* *151*

Chapter 28

Settling In: *Love Guides* *156*

Chapter 29

Being There: *Love Is Always There* *161*

Chapter 30

Bonding and Attachment: *Love Bonds* *166*

Chapter 31

Traveling Heavy: *Love Comforts* *171*

Chapter 32

Healing Love: *Love Welcomes* *176*

Chapter 33

No News or Good News? *Love Speaks* *181*

A LIFETIME FOR LOVE

Chapter 34
The "Blending" Family: *Love Grows* 189

Chapter 35
Tough Questions: *Love Is Truthful* 194

Chapter 36
A Language of Love: *Love Is Gentle* 199

Chapter 37
Meeting Needs: *Love Is Resourceful* 204

Chapter 38
Making You Mine: *Love Never Fails* 209

Appendix
Order for the Blessing of Parents and an Adopted Child 214

Introduction

For all who are led by the Spirit of God are children of God.
For you did not receive a spirit of slavery to fall back into fear,
but you have received a spirit of adoption. When we cry,
"Abba! Father!" it is that very Spirit bearing witness with our
spirit that we are children of God, and if children, then
heirs . . . of God and joint heirs with Christ. . . .

— ROMANS 8:14–17

In the Spring of 2002, my husband, Andrew, and I boarded a
plane to Moscow and then an overnight train to the city of Voronezh
in southern Russia. Two days later, a Russian judge declared that a
child we had met only three weeks before was our daughter. We
didn't know much of her language. We knew even less about her
past. We believed, however, that the God who made each of us
belong to him, could also teach us how to belong to one another.

1

This is my story, not our daughter's. Perhaps someday she will tell her own.

"Our Father, who art in heaven . . ." The words slip so easily past our lips, with so little hesitation, that there is not nearly enough time to consider what it is we are actually saying. On a hillside overlooking the Sea of Galilee, Jesus answered his eager disciples when they asked him how to pray. He taught them to begin by claiming God—the Eternal, Almighty Creator of all—as their father.

In that moment, Jesus gave us his Father as our own and initiated in us an entirely new life—even a new identity. But because only Jesus himself was begotten not made, because only he was *born* the Son of God, the rest of us must come to understand our identity as God's children in a different way. It is true that God creates every human being in his image, and, in that sense, we are all his children. But through Baptism, God brings us into a special relationship with him. The power of sacramental grace gives us a share in his divine life as the *adopted* children of the Father. We might as well pray, "Our (*adoptive*) Father."

Saint Paul tells us that the Spirit of God, the Holy Spirit, is the power behind our identity as children of God and coheirs with Christ. We are chosen, saved, loved, incorporated—even sealed (a legal term)—by the Holy Spirit, who then witnesses to us the truth of who we have become. That Spirit enables us to cry out to God, "*Abba*," or "Daddy." It is not a spirit of slavery or fear, but the *Spirit of adoption*.

The Holy Family shows us the depth of this mystery. We celebrate the birth of the baby Jesus at Christmas. We tend to overlook, however, that the Holy Family is both "biological" and "adoptive." Mary gave birth to Jesus, and Joseph adopted him. Taking Mary into his house, Joseph raised Jesus "as his own." But more, in doing so, Joseph gave himself fully to Jesus. Joseph's life reflects the divine fatherhood of God. He is not just a caregiver, but a father to the Word-made-flesh. His relationship to the child Jesus is not merely functional. It involves his identity, the core of who he is. Later on, the people of Nazareth would ask, "Isn't this the son of Joseph?" The answer may not be simple, but it cannot be a flat, "No."

The Church is also an adoptive "holy family." Each of us approaches the baptismal font as a creature and leaves it as a son or daughter of the Most High. We are adopted into the family of the Church. In Christ, people of every race and culture and age, otherwise unrelated to each other, are made brothers and sisters in one eternal household. The love of Christ challenges us to love one another well, to accept one another as part of the same family, to forgive and heal and care for each other, and to bear one another's burdens.

All this is to say that our Christian faith gives us, from its very beginnings, a rich source for reflecting on what adoption is and what it means. It is from our self-understanding as adopted children of God that we can begin to see what kind of love leads us to adopt a child ourselves, and what kind of love sustains us in being adoptive parents.

This book is written to encourage those who, like our family, are finding themselves walking a rather dimly lit road paved with many choices and few guideposts. Its purpose is to help families and their friends approach adoption from the perspective and calling of the Catholic faith. I have no intention of pushing adoption as an agenda. For, while almost all adoptive families consider themselves blessed, adopting a child is not right or appropriate for every family. I have, however, experienced the distinct call that adoption had—and continues to have—in our family life.

Because adoption doesn't just fall out of the sky, because every action that is taken flows from extended reflection and discernment,

I have begun each chapter with a spiritual reflection. This is followed by a personal anecdote drawn from our experience and the experiences of other families I have met, practical considerations, think-it-through-questions for those considering adoption and those who want to support them, and a brief prayer. It is my hope that any who are called to travel this path will experience the deeply spiritual nature of what they are doing and find in *Adoption: Room for One More?* a way to connect more deeply to the God whose love reaches far beyond himself to each one of us. This is the God we are privileged to call "Father."

Why Adopt?

CHAPTER 1

Called to Be Family

Choosing Love

So (Naomi) said, "See your sister-in-law has gone back to her people and to her gods; return after your sister-in-law." But Ruth said, "Do not press me to leave you or to turn back from following you! Where you go, I will go; where you lodge, I will lodge; your people shall be my people, and your God, my God.

— RUTH 1:15–16

REFLECTION

Ruth had a choice to make. Her husband was dead. Her sister-in-law, also widowed, had decided to go back to her original people and ways. And Naomi, her mother-in-law, was on the move as well. Free from any formal obligation, Ruth could choose any path without fear of judgment. There was no "wrong" choice. She was no longer bound to a husband or his family, nor was she tied to the world she had left when she married into another people. If she went back to Moab no one would blame her. Knowing what to expect—and what would be expected of her—Ruth could take her place among familiar surroundings, perhaps a little wiser for what she had experienced among foreigners.

But that is not what Ruth did. Instead of reaching back to erase what had happened to her, she chose to push ahead. Love would not let her return. The same love that had called her to marry outside her own people, now called her forward to accompany the mother-in-law who had embraced her. Love is always a choice—and always one that involves both a leaving behind and a going forth. Ruth chose not only to go with Naomi, but also to leave her own home, her own people, even her own gods behind. She could not have been sure of what the future would hold. Nonetheless, Ruth chose to make all that was Naomi's her own.

PERSONAL

The idea of adopting a child came to my husband and me gradually. Like land first appearing on the horizon, what we saw grew larger with every passing day, but it was impossible to see much detail. Far from shore, idealism was a ready companion. The realities of the process and the changes that adopting a child would bring to our lives were sketchy at best. With seven children, it was tempting to take a been-there-done-that attitude. (Kids are kids, right?) Still, we sensed that raising an adopted child might very well present us with a whole new set of challenges.

Looking back, we did not know what adopting a child would take, nor did we fully appreciate all that it would demand of us. One thing, however, was and still is very clear: adoption came to us as a distinct—and then sudden—call. One day we were just minding our own business. The next, we were inundated with adoption stories and information. Everything—even the readings at Mass—seemed to relate to adoption. When complete strangers started offering personal anecdotes, I began wondering if someone had stuck a sign on my back saying, "Talk to Me about Adoption."

As the seriousness of our considerations increased, the call to adopt became louder, clearer, and less avoidable. It was as if a path was being cleared before us. God, the divine Bushwhacker, was on the move. We just had to figure out how to follow—and keep up.

PRACTICAL

At the root, love is always and essentially *optional*. In many ways, the dynamic of adoption is a lot like that of marriage. When we choose to marry, we decide to love for life. We fully accept one another's strengths and weaknesses, choose to forgive, and commit to growth that brings us closer. A couple doesn't start off as one, but becomes one by becoming one another's. Marriage is a call, a vocation to self-giving love. It is not for everyone. The same things can be said of adoption.

Not infrequently, the spark of adoption originates with one spouse and then spreads to the other. In that case it is important to slow things down enough to allow *both* prospective parents time and space for discernment. You may be convinced beyond a doubt that God is calling you to adopt a child. There is no need to rush. The love required to build a strong family can be undermined if one spouse manipulates—or capitulates to—the other. The decision to adopt a child must be made in unity and in peace.

Many seem to consider adoption a generous or courageous choice. I do not. Recently I've been inspired by friends who discerned that adding an adoptive child to their family was not what God wanted. Their hearts were open; so were their ears. But as their children's needs changed and their own responsibilities evolved, things became clear. For them, the decision *not* to adopt was a choice to love that was made with both generosity and courage.

Adoption is the deliberate choice to extend the natural boundaries of family life. Stretching to make any family inclusive takes work. In our home, it did not happen all at once, but continues one step at a time. Those steps are daily choices that sometimes don't feel much like choices at all.

For reasons beyond our understanding, God chooses to be a Father to us. There is nothing that forces the Lord to do so. We are not the Master's only creatures, but God has not made himself a Father to stars or trees, butterflies or horses. We know this because the Son of God, Jesus Christ, became one of *us*. Every family is called to be what the household of heaven is: a haven of life and love. What we leave behind or press forward to in answering that call to adopt will never be a cookie-cutter or one-size-fits-all proposition. It will be as intensely personal as love itself.

Think it through

- How would adoption be choosing love for you and your family right now?

- How are you experiencing the idea of adopting a child as a calling from God?

- Are you ready to say "yes" to adoption? Are you free to be able to say "no"?

- Will you commit to praying daily for your friend or family member who is considering adoption?

Pray it through

HOLY SPIRIT, SPIRIT OF UNITY, help us to hear the call that draws us together. Empower us to choose love. Teach us how to belong to one another. Guide our considerations and our choices. Inspire us to look forward and beyond the boundaries of ourselves. Help us not only to know what you are asking of us, but also to follow it to completion. Keep our feet on the way of love and our hearts at the center of your will. Be with us, Holy Spirit, and with all the members of our family, those we know and love and those whom we have yet to meet. Amen.

CHAPTER 2

Moved By Gratitude

Love Turns Outward

When you give a luncheon or a dinner, do not invite your friends or your brothers or your relatives or rich neighbors, in case they may invite you in return and you would be repaid. But when you give a banquet, invite the poor, the crippled, the lame, and the blind. And you will be blessed because they cannot repay you, for you will be repaid at the resurrection of the righteous.

— LUKE 14:12–14

REFLECTION

God is the source of all goodness and the origin of every good thing we possess. Our food and shelter, our clothing—even our morning coffee—come from God. Knowing what we need even before we ask, the Lord provides for us. He does so every day, for our Creator is also our Sustainer.

When we realize how much we have to be grateful for, we also see that God cannot be repaid. We can, however, learn to give the way God does: without the expectation or even the possibility of being repaid. That is why Jesus tells us to invite those who are poor and sick to the parties we throw.

There are and always will be people in need. But when we set out along the path of gratitude, it doesn't take long for us to see that we are needy, too. On our own, we're not even capable of doing good. God is the fountain of every good deed we do. He wants us to be good because he wants us to be like him. Because God made us in his image, he knows that we are happy only to the extent that we render that image faithfully. He also knows that when we *are* good, we will *do* good for others.

PERSONAL

The summer before our youngest child turned two, my husband, Andrew, and I started wondering if she should remain our youngest child. We dared not tell anyone what we were thinking. With seven kids, we were already at the far edge of the societal galaxy. But even though raising seven children is a very full plate, something about our lives felt oddly incomplete. We just weren't done, and we knew it. In the process of thinking things through, two things became clear. Andrew and I had been more than blessed with a wonderful family, and there were children in this world who needed one.

But as we took stock of all that we could give, we also began to see what an adopted child could give us. Bringing a child into our family through adoption presented a marvelously challenging opportunity to live our faith and reach out with the works of mercy every day. At first we saw that adopting a child was something we could give to God in gratitude for all that the Lord had done for us. As time went on, it became clear that adopting a child was something God wanted to give to us.

PRACTICAL

Charity is love flowing in two directions. It takes a receptive giver and a generous receiver to find meaning in one another's loving actions. Adopting a child out of charity is not an unusual motivation. The challenge is to recognize that our motivations are often mixed and may not be as pure as we think or hope they are. In retrospect, I can see that some of what moved me to adopt a child was a bit tainted. I say "tainted" because perfect love is self-*less*. It does not take the self into account, not even the self's aspiration to be holy or do something good. Love always looks to the good of the other, and, because of that, neither pride nor pity has much to contribute to genuine charity.

We may start with pity for children who have no homes, but if pity remains the prime motivation for adoption, the child we adopt will never become a full or equal member of his or her own family. Feeling sorry for people interferes with our ability to love them. Actions flowing from guilt tend to bind rather than liberate; and bondage is not the same as bonding. If we overextend ourselves and try to give more than we are capable of giving, we create webs of interpersonal indebtedness. Resentment can find a home in the heart of the person who acts from a sense of doing good without fully weighing the cost. Every parent drinks from the cup of self-sacrifice. But I'll admit there are times I've allowed myself to become a bit too dependent on free refills!

Pride is another hindrance. Knowing the plight of orphaned children, many families who adopt wish that others would also consider adoption. But if we begin to applaud ourselves for doing something good, or hope that others will do so, we may be exchanging true charity for something that is more directed toward *ourselves* than it is toward *others*. More than a few people have told us that we are saints for adopting a child. While I wish becoming holy was that easy, I know it isn't. The truth is that when we adopted our daughter, we were only doing what we believe we had been led to do.

If gratitude and doing the right thing is what motivates you to adopt a child, you are not alone. But it is difficult to keep doing the right thing for the right reasons. All who take the risk to act in charity are likely to discover just how selfish we can be—and are. Genuine charity asks us to commit ourselves to growing in it daily and guarding it from those things that may endanger it. We can only do that if we set our hearts on the child we are choosing to love.

Think it through

- How do I already give back to others?
- Do I hope for or expect recognition for the good things I've done?
- How do I feel when I encounter weakness or poverty?
- How can an adoptive child's life be enriched by my presence?

Pray it through

HOLY SPIRIT, FIRE OF CHARITY, set our hearts ablaze. Work your love in our lives, your will in our plans, your holiness in our souls.

Teach us to desire what is good and right, and by your love, help us to bring your love to all. Keep us humble on the way. Protect us from pride and pity, from feeling that we are better, or more deserving, than anyone else. Inspire us to answer your call, and only your call, with prudence and patience. O Divine Flame, purify our motives and uproot everything in us that may be self-centered or self-serving. Perfect your love in us and through us. Lead us to those you intend for us to love as our own. Bless us and all our children with the warmth of your presence. Amen.

CHAPTER 3

Infertility

Love Gives Life

When Rachel saw that she bore Jacob no children, she envied her sister; and she said to Jacob, "Give me children, or I shall die!" Jacob became very angry with Rachel and said, "Am I in the place of God, who has withheld from you the fruit of the womb?"

— Genesis 30:1–3

REFLECTION

It is no wonder that Jacob's most-beloved Rachel suffered such intense pain and inner desperation over childlessness. Neither is it surprising that she became envious of her very fertile sister, Leah. Running to Jacob, Rachel begs him to give her children. For her, childlessness is death. Rachel will die if she is unable to perpetuate her life by giving life to a child. She is overwhelmed by the very real possibility of a future in which her worst fears will be realized.

Jacob responds to Rachel's anguish from the well of his own pain. He becomes angry. Startled by what he hears as an accusation that he has somehow withheld children from her, Jacob does not accept the blame for her infertility. Instead, he steps away from it and from her. God, he says, is responsible. If that isn't bad enough, Jacob then hints that there may be some reason God has not given Rachel children.

Apart from Jacob's anger and withdrawal, his response to Rachel is not completely without merit. All being and all life—both natural and supernatural—come from God. God is the origin and destiny of every living thing—the great Giver of gifts. Each of us is God's beneficiary. We have all received from heaven's abundance. The temptation, though, is to look at the Giver through the lens of what we want; that is, of what we do not yet have.

PERSONAL

Kara and John both felt called to marriage and family life, but had not yet found the right person until they found each other at a Catholic young adult group. They did not marry young, but they weren't old either. They both had jobs and apartments, nieces and nephews. Their love was an unmistakable answer to prayer. It was a love they both hoped to share with children, but after years of "trying," they realized that time was not on their side. Adoption seemed to be the only realistic option left. But with age not in their favor and many couples waiting years for a child, the prospect of being parents was anything but certain.

Emily, one of the teachers at our daughter's preschool, had been married for several years. She and her husband had been through just about everything to treat their infertility. Nothing worked. When she found out that our daughter had been recently adopted from Russia, Emily had all kinds of questions. For the three years our daughter attended that preschool, drop-off and pickup times provided a wonderful chance for the two of us to share our stories—and Emily's dream of being someone's mommy.

PRACTICAL

We have all known someone who struggles with infertility. But unless we have been there ourselves, we cannot know how deeply painful that struggle is, especially if it also involves the grief of miscarriage. Somewhere in the midst of the suffering an infertile couple bears, the notion of adopting a child may come to mind. Often, the idea is dismissed too hastily.

Some infertile couples feel that adopting a child is an admission of reproductive failure, but in truth, adoption is not a choice to give up on pregnancy. Many infertile couples who adopt eventually end up giving birth as well, as Emily and her husband did a few years after bringing their daughter home from China. Others, however, may see adoption as the acceptance of what they consider second-best or even as a last resort. Adoptive children, of course, are not inferior to "natural" ones. Both biological and adoptive parents think their children are the very best. And they're right!

On the other end of the spectrum are people—usually family members or friends—who view adoption as a ready "fix" to a couple's "problem." The choice to adopt, however, is both more and other than a "solution." It is a choice to welcome a child who under any other circumstance would not be part of your life.

Over time, focusing on what we don't have makes us unhappy with our lives as a whole. It also contributes to the mistaken notion that we are somehow entitled to whatever we want. The truth is that while we may intensely desire children, dream and hope and plan for them, no one has done anything to "deserve" them. Neither fertile nor infertile couples have a "right" to a child.

Children, on the other hand, do have legitimate claims on their parents. Every child has the right to be conceived in love; to be raised in a stable family; to have access to medical care, adequate food, and shelter; to be given an education; and to be formed in moral and spiritual truths. Sadly, we know that not all children will have what they need or deserve.

Human persons long to create as God does: to pass life on to others and to perpetuate who and what we are. Faith teaches us that one of the supreme gifts of marriage is children; that they are walking testimonies to married love. That is not said lightly or as if there were no other marital gifts. Still, marriage is so rich that to communicate the depth of that richness we must incarnate it. Husbands and wives give life to children as the living and eternal sign of marital love and self-gift.

While adoption may not "solve" anyone's "problem," it may well be an answer to a couple's prayers or the prayers of a homeless child. The challenge is letting go of what we do not have. If we can shift our focus from what it seems God is withholding from us, we can begin to glimpse—and then to receive—what he is offering. It is entirely possible that God, the giver of all life, is indeed giving children to those who are unable to give birth. It is also possible that God is giving families to children who need them. Adoption is one of the ways God chooses to answer those deep desires and needs.

Think it through

- ❧ Are there circumstances or relationships in which you've already acted in motherly or fatherly ways?

- ❧ Are you able to let go of your hopes for your family if they are not part of what God's plan is for you?

- ❧ Have you come to terms with the grief your infertility has caused, or do you still need more time to work through it?

- ❧ Do you see adopting a child more as a distinct calling or as a solution to your friend's or family member's problem?

Pray it through

HOLY SPIRIT, DIVINE COMFORTER, heal our wounds, comfort our grief, sustain us in hope. Keep our spirits from being clouded by disappointment. Help us to find life where we are, to treasure life wherever we find it, and to bring your everlasting life to all we meet. Teach us to be grateful for what you have given us already, and open our hearts to receive all that you wish to give us still. O Giver of Life, lead us according to your will. Enable us to recognize your answers to our prayers. Make our lives a nurturing womb, ready to receive, protect, and love. Watch over us and all the children you have given us: those here, in heaven, and any who await our embrace. Amen.

Who Should Adopt?

CHAPTER 4

The Opinion Poll

Love Encourages

For you are our father,
though Abraham does not know us
and Israel does not acknowledge us;
you, O LORD, are our father;
our Redeemer from of old is your name.

— Isaiah 63:16

REFLECTION

God mysteriously lays claim to every one of us. Every human being is, in reality, part of the whole human family. This holds true even in the face of those who would search for some reason to deny it. Each one of us can claim God as our Father. God's other children may not know or acknowledge us in any way. We ourselves may even

25

fail to recognize who we truly are. God, however, remains our Father nonetheless.

Things are not always what they seem to be, mostly because there is much we cannot see. Beneath the surface of our lives, however, is a flowing river of truth from which we can draw if we dare. Faith is our water jar. Entrusting ourselves to the God who sees everything helps us both to see things the way they are, and to imagine beyond what we see to the way things can be.

Personal

Ultimately, my husband, Andrew, and I both knew that in order for any adoption to succeed, we would have to get all the important people on board. Part of the challenge was to correctly discern just who was important and what weight to give to any individual's response. It took discipline not to share our snowballing excitement, but the effort during those four or five months was well worth it. A season of silence kept our own thinking focused and made it possible to be attentive to the thoughts and feelings that mattered most: those belonging to members of the family we already had.

We were convinced that if adopting a child was something that God was leading us to, we would hear the divine voice in the responses of the people closest to us. I remember gingerly raising the topic with my mother and grandmother, not really knowing where either of them would stand. Because they both lived with us, I knew that it would be unfair to simply inform them that we had decided to adopt. Instead, I confided in them.

Andrew and I then widened the circle of discernment to our children. Recognizing that any child we brought home would be one of them, we decided to grant each of our children the equivalent of veto power. Despite our growing desire, we were careful to reassure them that we would not move ahead with an adoption if any of them were truly opposed to it.

We talked with each of our kids individually and asked them to join us in the decision process. Some of them asked important questions and took time to think things through. Others couldn't jump on the adoption bandwagon fast enough. We encouraged them to share any concerns they had, and we listened to every point they raised. If honest opposition or discomfort was voiced within our own family, we were prepared to interpret it as a heavenly red light to what we were considering. What we got was one green light after another.

We didn't go public with our intention to adopt until we knew that our whole family was of one mind in support of it. When we did, we were surprised by the reactions we received. Sufficient support was not hard to find, but it was not always where we thought we would find it. Some people told us about their own family adoption stories; others just listened to our plans with a smile. Still others offered concrete and much-appreciated help.

There was another group of people, however, quick to pass on every adoption horror story they had ever heard. One woman told me about a family that had adopted a girl from Korea who turned out to be mentally ill. Another recounted a story of an adopted boy who was abusive toward other children in the family. Quite a few people observed that adopted children never really fit into their families, that they *all* have emotional issues, and that most of them are disabled in some way. With great conviction they shared many of their own fears and prejudices. Alarmed at first, we came to realize that most of what these people offered us flowed from a mixture of genuine concern and simple ignorance.

Practical

No adoption plan meets with universal acclaim or universal opposition, but opinions can and do change. Every family who chooses to adopt understandably longs to share their expectant joy with family and friends. Not everyone, however, will immediately embrace the path. There are people in your life who can run alongside you with abandon. Some can join you for only part of the way. Others, for reasons of their own, will not be able to join you at all. Eventually, we are able to identify the people with whom we can comfortably share our journey, as well as those with whom we cannot. Most are happy to come along, or at least watch, in joy.

Faith teaches us to gaze rather than glance. It gives us vision that is more than human, vision that is a glimpse of how God sees things—not twenty/twenty, but eternity/eternity. Our world, however, is full of people who need glasses. That is why the choice to adopt a child meets with a varied and plentiful response. It may be liberating to know that a person's reaction to your plan to adopt does not have to be a litmus test for your relationships.

In dealing with other people's opinions, we discovered that, perhaps more than any other quality, adoption demands imagination. Adoption requires us to recognize and act on something we cannot see; namely, that there is a child somewhere who is meant to be ours. Not everyone around us is able to visualize things in that way.

Think it through

⁕ Whose support and encouragement has surprised you?

⁕ What is one potentially valuable thing you have heard from someone who was negative about your interest in adopting a child?

* Who are the "important people" in your life, those whose support you really need in order to adopt a child?

* How can you voice a concern you may have about the interest your friends or family members have in adoption in a way that still supports and encourages them?

Pray it through

HOLY SPIRIT, SPIRIT OF UNDERSTANDING, speak your will clearly in our hearts. Give us the ability to imagine, to trust what we cannot yet see, and to walk by faith. O Heavenly Comforter, send us all the encouragement we need. Guard the joy you have given us from the words of those who cannot share it. Uphold us as your children, and teach us to affirm your will in others' lives, even when we don't understand it. Be with us until our journey ends, and befriend the children who wait for us. Amen.

CHAPTER 5

Not For Everyone

Love Listens

Unless the Lord builds the house,
those who build it labor in vain.

— Psalm 127:1

"For which of you, intending to build a tower, does not first sit down and estimate the cost, to see whether he has enough to complete it?"

— Luke 14:28

Reflection

Our Catholic faith teaches us to give God's plan preeminence over our agendas. That principle applies as much to his plan for our families as it does to everything else. God created the family and he has a plan for every family. If we want our families to honor God, we have to let him be the architect and the general contractor. The truth is that when we get involved in all the details, we are attempting to wrestle the whole project away from God's control. And honestly, anything that is out of *God's* control is just plain out-of-control!

Plans, though, require planning. We all know that in order to have a beautiful wedding, a great surprise birthday party, or a successful opening of a new store, logistics and details need to be thoroughly considered and thought out. But somehow, when it comes to planning our family lives, we are tempted to leave our brains outside our front doors and tell ourselves that love is the only thing we need. Such notions aren't just unrealistic; they are entirely contrary to our faith. Jesus instructs his disciples to count the cost of their discipleship, to honestly think through what they are undertaking by following him. Jesus does this not because he doesn't want disciples, or because he is trying to tell them that following him is a bad idea. It is because real love is not opposed to real thinking. God created our hearts and minds to work together.

Adopting a child is very much like building the tower Jesus was talking about in the Gospel. Once you've decided to move forward, it is important to consider whether or not you have what is needed to complete the task. It is also important to make a conscious choice to *follow* the process God has set before us, and not lead it. We are wiser if we do so, realizing that not everyone can or should adopt a child. Adoption is *not* for everyone. There is no shame in coming to realize that it isn't the right choice for you or your family.

Personal

As we began our adoption journey, my husband and I did our best to assess just what we were actually able to take on. With seven children already, we knew that there were children whose needs we just weren't equipped to handle. As much as we wanted to adopt, we knew that adopting a child who had needs we could not meet would have been imprudent *and* unloving. We made the decision early on not to knowingly do anything that would compromise our freedom along the path to adoption. We promised ourselves, each other, and our whole family that we would only take the next step in the process if we were completely ready to do so. Until that was the case, we were prepared to wait. If the next step was not something we could do in peace and good conscience, we were prepared to withdraw from the process entirely and accept that adoption was not for us, at least not at the time.

PRACTICAL

While you may have all the right reasons, motivations, and resources, adoption may still not be right for you—or for a child. If your marriage is struggling, or you are at the limit of what you can handle, it is wise to fully consider those things and to be open to reconsidering the whole undertaking. Families should also weigh the possibility that while they may be called to adopt a child, now may not be the right time. You will find your path by listening to both your hearts and your heads.

But listening can be a tricky business. Who you listen to and how you listen has great influence on what you will hear. As Catholics, we are called to listen to the guidance of God in prayer, hear what the Church teaches with the intent to follow it, ask the advice of the people who love us, and take direction from the realities of our life circumstances. Above all, we are bound to fully recognize that every child who is available for adoption has rights that must be placed ahead of the desires of prospective parents.

While many well-meaning homosexuals seek to adopt, our Church teaches that the best interests of a child are not served by being adopted by a homosexual couple. It is not that homosexual persons are incapable of loving children or of raising them well. That is certainly not the case. What the Church teaches, though, is rooted in the belief that every person has the right to a family that is formed as God intended it to be. Children not only need—they have a right to—a mother *and* a father. Only marriage understood as the communion of male and female can be the foundation of a family in which both motherly and fatherly love are given and received.

This teaching, along with the Church's very cautious endorsement of single-parent adoption, is more difficult to understand in the current culture than it used to be. Ours is a society of cohabitation and divorce where the ideal of family life is hard to find. Ours is a culture that promotes a fluid definition of marriage, family, even gender. In the midst of these, our Church challenges us to show preferential treatment to the poor, the weak, and the young, and chooses to proclaim what we owe to children.

As Catholics, we may struggle with the teachings of our faith, while we aspire to live them in both love and prudence. If we approach family life from the perspective of Catholic belief, every one of us will find ourselves challenged.

Think it through

- Are you a willing listener? Whose voice do you listen to the most?

- How is your interest in adoption part of living your faith?

- Would you be able to step away from the adoption process if you became convinced that it was not the right choice for your family at this time?

✎ Are you placing any expectations on a friend or family member that might pressure them in any way?

Pray it through

HOLY SPIRIT, SPIRIT OF PRUDENCE AND LOVE, guide us in discernment. Show us how to live our faith fully in family life. Help us to place our desires and hopes into your hands. O Wisdom, teach us to recognize your voice in what we hear, and grant us the grace to listen attentively. Help us to follow and not lead, to approach every aspect of our lives with the desire to live according to your plan. Give us the grace to fully consider the journey ahead of us and the humility to understand and accept your will for us and for all children who need families. Amen.

CHAPTER 6

Special Challenges

Love Discerns

"In you the orphan finds mercy."

—Hosea 14:3

"My grace is sufficient for you, for power is made perfect in weakness."

—2 Corinthians 12:9

Reflection

Saint Paul was a one-of-a-kind, brilliantly inspired evangelist. Once he met the Risen Lord personally, Paul put every gift and talent, every moment of his life into the mission of the Gospel. He founded many churches all over the Roman Empire. His letters to the churches he founded form the majority of the New Testament.

Paul traveled and preached tirelessly. He endured shipwrecks, trials, persecution, prison, ridicule, and hardship. Saint Paul had a lot to offer, and he offered it all.

But in Paul's quest to spread the Gospel of Jesus Christ, he suffered what he refers to as a "thorn in the flesh." This difficulty so hampered him that he begged God three times to remove it. God did not. Instead, God told Paul that his power was most visible in Paul's weakness.

PERSONAL

While singles may feel like a fifth wheel at times, God has no less a plan for their lives than he does for the lives of married couples. That plan occasionally includes opening one's life to a child through foster care or even adoption. Gianna had been a successful big band vocalist for years. When she decided to stop touring and settle down, she opened her heart and adopted two children from Central America. Raising her son and daughter on her own hasn't always been easy for Gianna. Her dedication and complete gift of self, however, have inspired many who know her to lend support.

Age is another concern. John and Kara were older than most people are when they have children biologically. When they decided to pursue adoption, several people told them that they probably wouldn't have the energy to take care of a baby. They are, however, secure and well-established both as individuals and as a couple. Their age makes them able to offer the kind of stability every child relies on. The fact that they really have been there and done that means they have no inner conflicts about putting their own plans or interests on the back burner for the sake of their son.

PRACTICAL

There is no typical profile of the adoptive parent. All kinds of people in many different situations adopt children. We may have what authorities deem adequate. Still, we all have weaknesses and limitations. None of us fully exemplifies the ideal. On the other hand, all of us have gifts as well, even those single, older, or disabled adults who seek to adopt a child.

The singles I know have a degree of personal freedom that can enable them to make their lives a radical gift of service in love. They are often the ones who fill in the gaps, who are available in a pinch, who are willing and able to step into the breach when no one else can or will. Similarly, older adults are usually more financially and personally secure than their younger counterparts. The kind of stability they can offer an adoptive child is a precious and life-changing gift.

If you are a single person seeking a way to live a life of love and self-gift, adopting a child is a beautiful way to do that. And although children need both a mother and a father, one loving parent is certainly better than none. That being said, the single parent must be willing to sacrifice the personal freedom he or she is used to in order to raise a child and to develop a network of go-to people who can listen and help.

If you are an "older" couple hoping to share the life and love you've built together, adoption is one way of doing just that. While parenting does demand energy, wisdom that comes from experience is valuable, too. Older parents should, however, make an effort to keep up with the world their child is growing up in.

God made us to be walking works of his mercy. If we are following God's call in our lives, God will give *through* us. We will not be limited to giving only what we ourselves have to give. God will make our lives capable of passing on to others the merciful love we have received from him. The Holy Spirit inspires us to obtain mercy by acting mercifully.

Many of us practice the works of mercy—both corporal and spiritual—right in our own homes. Every day parents clothe the naked, feed the hungry, instruct the ignorant, and admonish little sinners who, at times, commit not-so-little sins! Family life and love calls each member to treat all the others with mercy.

Every child deserves a loving family; not every child has one. Somewhere in the world there is a child who is alone. That loneliness can be healed by an act of mercy, by an offering of both gifts and limitations. Your willingness to give your life to a child in need makes the world a place where people can encounter God's mercy in one another.

The necessary evaluation that is part of the adoption process can make it difficult to remember that "perfect" parents don't exist any more than "perfect" children do. Nobody really has, or is, or does it all. When it comes to relationships, however, the important question is less about what or how much is lacking and more about what another person can and will find in us. God knows how to use our weaknesses as effectively as he uses our strengths.

Think it through

- ❧ What weaknesses in yourself or others have you seen God use?
- ❧ Are you willing to give up personal freedom in order to raise a child?
- ❧ What can you do now to develop a strong support system for an adoptive child?

✦ Is there something specific you can offer your friend or family member to help fill in any gaps they may have?

Pray it through

HOLY SPIRIT, SPIRIT OF COUNSEL AND STRENGTH, I come to you with a willingness to serve. I have heard your call to make myself a total gift. Now I ask you to show me how and to whom I should give myself. Strengthen my commitment to love not only in theory, but in daily reality. Teach me to embrace self-sacrifice with joy, to give freely all that I am, all the gifts and limitations I have. Direct me to those whose support I will need, and give me the grace to ask for help and to receive it. Perfect your power in my weakness. Bless the children you have called me to love with the richness of mercy you have inspired in me. Amen.

Choices

CHAPTER 7

Pink or Blue?

Love Affirms

May our sons in their youth
be like plants full grown,
our daughters like corner pillars,
cut for the building of a palace.

— Psalm 144:12

Reflection

Our Creator equips each one of us to become what he designed us to be. Masculinity or femininity is part of how God does that. At the beginning of creation, God designed humanity to be male and female. Thus, from our very origins we express a divinely given complementarity. Men and women together bear the image of God.

God indeed loves all his children, both sons and daughters. Masculine and feminine, the Lord delights in us all.

There is nothing haphazard about how we are created. We are intended to be exactly who we are. There are no assembly lines in heaven, no conveyor belts on which souls are randomly injected into bodies. God has a plan for every single one of us. It is with that plan in mind that each of us is made.

Whether our children are boys or girls—or boys *and* girls!—we want to see all of them reach their potential. All parents look for areas in which their children excel. We readily notice that a child can catch a ball or sing on pitch. It may be more challenging, however, to identify the portion of every child's giftedness that lies hidden in his or her gender. While our culture accepts that both boys and girls can grow up to be firefighters or teachers, we sometimes overlook the things that belong to us simply because we are male or female. These attributes flow from the essence of who we are and not what we do. A girl may grow up to be an excellent mother, and a boy may become a caring father. These roles are not interchangeable. They are complementary by design. God intends them to be so.

While both have attempted to do so, neither gender can claim divine preference. The Scriptures are full of godly men and godly women. Although biblical cultures were largely patriarchal, there are plentiful stories celebrating women for their heroism and holiness. Some—like Deborah and Esther—exercised leadership in the community, while others found their vocations in other less visible roles. The same can be said of men of God.

Personal

We decided to request a little girl very early in formulating our plan to adopt. Our reasoning was simply a matter of balance.

Because our youngest daughter was preceded by two older brothers, and because the next sister up the ladder was seven years older, we thought it would be best to add more pink to the mix. Intentionally surrounding our youngest daughter with brothers was not something that seemed particularly appealing—or fair. From our point of view, she needed a sister.

Our daughters, of course, were thrilled; our sons, less so. They had hoped that our plan to adopt would help them to get even, that is, balance our family's ratio of boys to girls. Accepting our rationale, however, they resigned themselves to a final score of boys: 3, girls: 5. In the end, they recognized that the choice was not nearly as important for them as it was for their youngest sister.

PRACTICAL

All parents dream about their future children. When we do, we imagine them looking and acting in particular ways. Gender preferences often shape the mental images we create. Many mothers happily anticipate dressing up their little girls in velvet with ruffly tights and black patent leather shoes. More than a few fathers, on the other hand, are just as eager to imagine fishing or playing catch with their sons. When I think about it, before I had children I pictured them all as golden-haired girls with green eyes and larger-than-average noses running barefoot through fields of tall grass. Not one of our eight fits that description—except, of course, for the bare feet.

The relationships our families share and build are influenced but not determined by gender. Mothers and daughters have a different kind of relationship than do mothers and sons. Likewise, the dynamic between fathers and sons is quite distinct from what develops between fathers and their daughters. I can attest from my own experience that brothers and sisters deal with each other in ways as different as night and day.

Gender is one of the choices adoptive parents can make but birth parents cannot. Being able to exercise an option, however, doesn't necessarily mean that it is best to do so. There are many reasons to adopt a boy, and an equal number of reasons to adopt a girl. Ultimately, prospective parents must decide whether they have a good reason to choose either. Numerous adoptive families choose to remain open to either a boy or a girl.

That being said, there is nothing wrong with choosing the gender of the child you will adopt. People do exercise the gender option for all kinds of reasons. Some, having fond memories of an older brother, choose to adopt a boy first. Others believe that they will be better prepared to raise a daughter than a son—or the opposite. Families with tight living quarters may select one gender over another so that their children can share a room.

The most important consideration regarding the gender of your adopted child is determining just how important having a son or daughter is. Gender is an area in which a family is able to allow a degree of flexibility. The path, while broad at the beginning, must eventually narrow toward a commitment to a particular child. Selecting the gender of a child—or deciding not to do so—will lead parents down one fork in the road ahead.

Think it through

✤ Have you decided to choose the gender of your adoptive child? If so, what motivated your choice?

✤ What is the thing you most look forward to in raising your daughter or son?

❧ What do you think is the greatest challenge of raising boys or girls today?

❧ Are you particularly attached to your family member or friend adopting a boy or a girl?

Pray it through

HOLY SPIRIT, GIFT OF THE MOST HIGH, teach us to recognize the beauty of all that you have given us. Help us to rejoice not only in similarities, but in differences. Give us a true appreciation for your call to us as men and as women. Dispel our suspicions. Enlighten our minds. Dispose our hearts toward one another in love. Heal the hurts we may have suffered in unhealthy relationships, as well as those we may have caused to others. Show us how to embrace our children fully as the sons and daughters you have given us. Keep us always close to the heavenly Father we share and in whose image we were created. Amen.

CHAPTER 8

How Old Are You?

Love Believes

If any of you is lacking in wisdom, ask God, who gives to all generously and ungrudgingly, and it will be given to you.

— JAMES 1:5

REFLECTION

World literacy is at its highest level in human history, and people are more educated than they have ever been. But somehow, we don't seem to be any smarter. Perhaps it's because we need something more than mere knowledge. We need wisdom. Wisdom is the power to know if, when, and how to use the knowledge we have gained. Wisdom helps us discern what is genuinely important.

As much as we try to avoid it, our lives are full of decisions. The choices we make ought to be based on something more substantial than a game of eeny meeny miney moe. Hopefully, the values we hold and the principles we maintain guide us in the decisions we make every day. We are wise when we do more than just live; we are wise when we know *how* to live.

Still, human life is full of confusion and uncertainty. We have all experienced times in which we truly had no idea what we should do. Lacking wisdom, however, is no cause for worry. All we have to do is ask God for help. Our all-knowing and all-wise Father will give us wisdom. Notice, though, that the Lord does not promise us the wisdom we need—but only the wisdom we ask for. God wants us to *ask*.

Personal

For us, the most confounding aspect of the adoption process involved our daughter's age. Meeting nearly three-year-old Yulia at a "Baby House" in Voronezh, Russia, suddenly made everything about adopting a child difficult and confusing. She didn't look much like the "baby" we had planned to add to our family. She was older than any child we had envisioned adopting.

Resisting the inclination to move on, we asked God to make his will clear to us. After a few days—and a whole lot of e-mail traffic back and forth from home—we became quite convinced that Yulia was meant to be our daughter. In the end, our choice was between choosing the "right" age or the "right" child. Our youngest daughter would hold her position at the end of the line. Without knowing it, we already had our family's "baby."

In retrospect, I don't know why we struggled over our adoptive daughter's age as much as we did. Sure, it's been a bit confusing to explain how sisters can be five months apart and in different grades at school, and none of us have ever been quite sure how to respond

when someone asks if they are twins. But we've all had a bit of fun
with the answers we give!

PRACTICAL

To choose an adoptive child's age is essentially to make a choice
between "history" and "mystery." The most difficult part of making a
choice about age is the lack of information about how either choice
might play out. On one hand, an infant may appear to present adoptive parents with more of a "blank slate," that is, less of a past to con-
tend with. But a baby may also bring unrevealed challenges that
parents did not expect to address. In contrast, an older child has a past
that should not—and really cannot—be ignored. When a child has
more of a "past," the effects of that past are often more visible.

Age plays a larger role in adoption than one might guess. It is one
of the first dominos in a long sequence of cause and effect that is
relevant to much that an adoptive family will address in time.
Health, development, emotional well-being, and the dynamics of
family relationships can all be influenced by a child's age at
adoption.

Age is an important piece of information in evaluating a child's
health, partly because there are several medical conditions that cannot be diagnosed in young infants. Furthermore, the care a child is
receiving may make it difficult to tell the difference between tem-
porary developmental delays and long-term disabilities.

While adoption is in the long-term best interest of a child, it is
an enormous—even traumatic—emotional transition. The tools a
child has to adjust are largely determined by his or her level of development. Age may also be a factor in how a child will address adoption later in life. Children brought home during infancy have no

living memory of a personal past before adoption. While some parents may consider this an advantage, many children do not. The inability to connect to the past can become a recurring theme in some children's lives. Slightly older children may remember their birth parents or orphanage life in detail. For some of them, the memories are comforting; for others, they are an ongoing source of fear and anxiety.

A child's age at the time of adoption may also influence how a family's children relate to one another. Adoption makes it possible to bring an older brother or sister into the mix or place a new child between children already in the home.

In truth, no child is a completely fresh canvas, but no child's future is totally determined by his or her past. Your child's age comes as a package of both challenges and gifts. The unknowns of adopting an infant may be a bit frightening; the difficult past bound to an older child may seem daunting. Somehow, however, the challenges of both history and mystery fade in the eyes of a child who has waited—however long—to be part of a loving family.

Think it through

- Are you more comfortable with "mystery" or "history"?

- What can you do now to begin gathering the resources you'll need to help your child process his or her adoption later on?

- What are your reasons for planning to adopt a baby, toddler, or older child?

- What can you do to reassure your friend or family member about the uncertainties and unknowns they will face with their adoptive child?

Pray it through

HOLY SPIRIT, SPIRIT OF WISDOM, you know all that has passed and all that will be. Guide us along the path you desire us to take. Give us the wisdom we need and the courage to ask for it when we need it. Help us to discern what is right for our family. Keep us from trying to carry what is too heavy for us. Teach us to commend everything and everyone into your hands. Reassure us in what we do not or cannot know. Sustain us in all that we do know, but do not have the power to change. Fill us with gratitude for the gifts you have given our children, as well as for the challenges that accompany those gifts. Bless the children you have chosen to be ours, and make us a blessing to them for the rest of their lives. Amen.

CHAPTER 9

Cross-Racial and Cross-Cultural Adoption

Love Stretches

Do not fear, for I am with you;
I will bring your offspring from the east,
and from the west I will gather you;
I will say to the north, "Give them up,"
and to the south, "Do not withhold;
bring my sons from far away,
and my daughters from the end of the earth—
everyone who is called by my name,
whom I created for my glory,
whom I formed and made."

— Isaiah 43:5–7

Reflection

The Holy Spirit is a Spirit of unity and love. That love has no borders or boundaries of any kind. From every direction, every place, every culture and language and race God calls us as one people—simply because we belong to the Lord.

Diversity is both a fact of life and the beauty of creation. Truly celebrating the richness of our differences, however, is not as simple or as easy as it sounds. While most of us relish the great variety of flowers and landscapes and birds, many of us have felt intimidated at times by diversity that is purely human. I may be comfortable talking about how people come in all shapes, colors and sizes. But all that philosophy does little to make me feel comfortable when I walk into a room where I'm the one who is "different."

God, however, has another point of view. Our Creator has made every one of us for divine glory. Each of us is tailor-made, made to fit. There is no doubt that we belong. But like pieces in a puzzle, our differences are what help us to discover where we belong—not just with God, but with one another.

Personal

Al and Mary embraced this perspective long before the culture at large did. They had not been able to have biological children and were open to adopting children from different backgrounds. As a result, their family included two Caucasian children, an Asian child, and two Latino children. While they readily admit that they had little idea of the challenges they would face at the time, theirs is a story of love without boundaries and a generosity of heart that testifies to the unconditional love God has for each one of us.

PRACTICAL

More and more adoptive families have chosen to make cultural and racial differences less and less a factor in the decisions they make. Some have made race a primary concern and have actively sought to build multiracial families. Others have accepted referrals for children of races other than their own even when they had not expected to do so.

Families who choose to adopt cross-racially or cross-culturally have a special set of considerations. It is important for all of us to recognize that racism does (still!) exist, and that the cross-racial adoptive family may well encounter it. Parents who have never had to worry about prejudice may be surprised to find just how pervasive it is. Some may even experience it in members of their own extended families.

The tragedy of race discrimination affects individual children differently. For some, a racial difference between them and their parents or siblings is not an issue. For others, race looms large on the child's interpersonal horizon. An adopted minority child may project perceived racism onto situations in which it does not actually play a role. I know of one little girl who incorrectly concluded that she was not given the part she hoped for in a dance recital only because she is Chinese.

There is one additional point that parents considering cross-racial adoption should bear in mind. An obvious distinction in race between a child and his or her other family members means that the adoption itself cannot be kept private. The cross-racially adopted child does not have the luxury of choosing if—or when—to tell others that he became a member of his family through adoption. Having such a personal matter made common knowledge can be a lot for children and their parents to carry. But together, parents and their children can turn their situation into an opportunity to witness to ever-broadening love.

The cross-cultural aspects of adoption are distinct from racial matters. Even children who are of the same race as their adoptive parents can come from a radically different cultural background. Welcoming any child into your family means welcoming an entire history and heritage as well. Part of the joy of adoption is widening our cultural awareness and horizons. There are no ethnic requirements for enjoying refried beans, borscht, or lo mein.

There are many ways for parents to keep an adopted child connected to his or her culture of origin. Native foods, music, language, and crafts can all be given a place of honor. Al and Mary have gone to all kinds of local community cultural festivals. And yes, they've learned a bit of Spanish along the way. I also know a foster family who has welcomed numerous children from all kinds of racial and cultural backgrounds. The mother is Lithuanian, the father Syrian; their four children have brothers and sisters who are Cambodian, Vietnamese, and African American.

Highlighting a child's background affirms that child's identity and self-understanding. Cultural pride and connectedness is especially helpful to children who were adopted beyond infancy. For them, familiar foods, stories, songs, and artistic expression can provide an irreplaceable source of comfort and belonging.

Culture sharing affords families a rich avenue of mutual acceptance. Such exploration and exchange can flow joyously in two directions. I will never forget the absolute ecstasy our daughter expressed when she tried on the little Russian national costume I had bought for her. She was even more delighted when I tried mine on, too! Families who do what they can to participate in their child's culture should also feel free to fully share their own heritage. They should do so regardless of the child's racial or ethnic background.

Our Russian daughter has competed in Irish step-dancing at the world championship level. It is not uncommon to see more than a few Asian girls dance the jig as well!

Think it through

- Are you open to adopting a child from a race or culture very different from your own?

- How do you intend to handle the questions people you know and don't know will ask?

- What things can you do to share your own culture and heritage with your child and connect your child with his or her culture and heritage?

- Can you identify any prejudice or racism in your own heart that might undermine your support of your friend or family member's plan to adopt?

Pray it through

HOLY SPIRIT, LORD OF ALL NATIONS, give us eyes that see the beauty of every culture and race. Stretch our hearts beyond the boundaries of birth, nation, and race, and help us to fully welcome your image in all people. Help us to see the unity that lies deeper than all diversity. Enculturate your eternal kingdom in our hearts, where all are recognized as sons and daughters of the Father. Root out any racism that may linger in our souls, and give us the strength to act justly when we encounter it ourselves. Through the life we share with our children, reaffirm that love has no color, race, or nationality. Show us how to belong to one another and to you. Amen.

CHAPTER 10

Special Needs Adoption

Love Lifts

I delivered the poor who cried,
and the orphan who had no helper. . . .
I was a father to the needy,
and I championed the cause of the stranger.

— Job 29:12, 16

For everything created by God is good, and nothing is to be
rejected, provided it is received with thanksgiving . . .

— 1 Timothy 4:4

REFLECTION

Everything God creates is good. God plans, fusses, and labors to
bring about our world. He fills it with variety beyond our

imaginations. Sights and sounds, smells and tastes, textures and temperatures—all our senses testify to the magnificence of creation. The divine Master Craftsman does not waste his eternity making anything substandard. Each day in that first week of creation, God looked at his work and saw goodness in all of it. We, however, may have some trouble doing that. Because we do not see things with God's eyes, we fail to appreciate the goodness—the "godness"—that encircles us.

Most people have no difficulty putting trees and animals, beaches and lakes, mountains and seasons into the plus column. But when we get to people, we suddenly lose that ability. There are things about ourselves and each other that we would not accept if we didn't have to. When those line items reach beyond our thresholds of tolerance, many of us reject them by rejecting the person who is attached to them.

PERSONAL

The very first adoption form we filled out, our agency's initial application, asked us to list any kinds of special needs that we would be willing to accept in a child. I was somewhat surprised at what was on the list of disabilities. Crossed eyes, a cleft palate or lip, a missing finger or toe; some of these things seemed rather small. But there were also things on that list I considered enormous—things like autism, deafness, Hepatitis C, cerebral palsy, and HIV.

Honestly, the special needs question frightened me. On one hand, I felt guilty for wanting a healthy child. On the other hand, Andrew and I knew that we did not have the resources to commit ourselves to major, ongoing medical challenges. Problems that could be corrected with medical intervention, mild to moderate learning disabilities, or a background that included extreme poverty, abuse, or neglect was as much as we could handle.

Practical

The list of what can be considered "special needs" is very long indeed. Likewise, the range of conditions and diagnoses is enormous. Some of these constitute the full explanation for why a particular child is available for adoption. Birth parents may not have either the personal and financial resources or support necessary to address their child's needs. Sometimes children with correctable "defects" are abandoned to the streets, especially in cultures that are superstitious about such things.

Every child is good and worthy of life and love. Those words come easily when we envision healthy children; kids who can run and play and learn to read; children that are easy to be proud of. But such words don't always flow like milk from a bottle. While most of us have a sense of compassion for families who find themselves suddenly facing challenges they did not anticipate, few can even begin to understand parents who would deliberately seek to adopt a child whose future is not brimming with possibilities.

Happily, there are waiting lists for those who are willing to adopt children with Down's syndrome and spina bifida. Beneath the surface, it is not difficult to see why. Families who seek to parent a child with special needs do so because they trust that among the thorny challenges they face are rare and fragrant gifts. The children they are called to adopt may be among the poorest and neediest, often those who have no one willing to help them. Whether through life experience or expertise, parents of children with special needs know the value of small accomplishments and the depth of simple joys. For them, a child taking his first steps at six years of age is as exciting— maybe more exciting—than a baby walking across the kitchen on her first birthday.

Parents of children with special needs, by either birth or adoption, are expert at separating the human condition from the human person. They do not view their children as burdens or disappointments. Many are deeply grateful for challenges most of us hope to avoid. One mother of a child with special needs told me her daughter had made her a better person. Accepting a child another couple had refused as "too defective," her family had learned to look past their daughter's prognosis. While this little girl takes seven medications a day to manage multiple challenges, her family has been able to rejoice in her gifts. To them, she is a loving daughter and big sister, a creative, artistic, and fearless child.

Those who have completed special-needs adoption recommend that prospective parents have strong support systems, both personal and professional. They stress the importance of learning not only about their child's medical realities, but also about available educational resources and services. Figuring out how to navigate the system and identify advocates for your child before coming home will empower you to address your child's needs more effectively.

There are no "perfect" children, just as there are no "perfect" parents. If your heart is open to adopting a child with serious medical or developmental challenges, you are a very special person indeed. The desire to adopt a child with special needs is an inspiration of the Holy Spirit. God, however, does not ask us to do anything that lies beyond our capabilities. Our heavenly Father gives support to what we seek within the divine will. Charity is never imprudent; but love is at times extravagant. It is that kind of over-the-top, extravagant self-gift that enables the members of these special families to receive one another with thanksgiving and joy.

Think it through

- ❧ Is there something in your own experience or expertise that leads you to consider adopting a child with special needs?

- ❧ What can you do before your adoption to educate yourself about your child's medical challenges and acquire the best available resources to address your child's needs and your own?

- ❧ What impact will adopting a special needs child have on the rest of your family?

- ❧ What can you do now to become comfortable with people who share the needs your friend's or family member's adoptive child has?

Pray it through

HOLY SPIRIT, AUTHOR OF ALL GOOD, help us to be faithful to the calling you have placed in our hearts. Guide the choices we make in our lives so that they affirm the beauty and dignity of every human life. Help us to see your image in everyone we meet. Teach us to value one another for who we are rather than for what we are able to do. Open our hearts without fear to the weak. Empower us to love our children as they come to us and to embrace their challenges as our own. Give us great joy in small things. Seal us with both prudence and generosity that we would live within our means, but withhold nothing from you or the children who will become ours. Amen.

CHAPTER 11

Adopting More Than One Child?

Love Multiplies

"May God almighty bless you and make you fruitful and numerous, that you may become a company of peoples."

— GENESIS 28:3

See, I and the children whom the LORD has given me are signs and portents in Israel from the LORD of hosts, who dwells on Mount Zion.

— ISAIAH 8:18

REFLECTION

Being created in the divine image, our lives are meant to be heavily laden with luscious and plentiful fruit. Even in the very beginning, God speaks of multiplying, not simply adding. The intention of the Father is very clear: we are to be fruitful and numerous, a "company of peoples." Almost every ancient blessing regarding family life contains a prayer for unparalleled fruitfulness.

That is because our God is one of abundance matched by magnificent generosity. He never wavers in his desire to give. When the Lord sees the conditions in which we live, the unmet needs we have, and our hunger for love, God does indeed want to adopt every one of us.

But we can find it frightening to allow ourselves to become vulnerable to a God who wants to give us so much. We may not want to feel indebted or obligated. Similarly, we may be afraid of being overwhelmed by such a torrent of gifts. Whatever our rationale, the result is that very few of us ever accept all that God longs to give.

This reticence to receive can be very clearly seen in our society. Most of today's families are carefully planned, so much so that some are practically made to order. The question is: *whose* order? Complete openness to the gift of life through marriage is not the cultural norm. It is, however, the call of our Catholic faith.

PERSONAL

Before we traveled to Russia to find a child, our friends predicted that we would want to take home every child we met. With a firm grasp on the realities of what we could do, that wasn't how we experienced it. Adopting more than one child was a concept not even close to being on our radar screen.

Stopping over in Germany on our first trip, however, we met a couple who told us quite matter-of-factly that they were on their way to pick up the three children they had decided to adopt. Two of them were biological siblings; all three were younger than the ten-year-old son who was traveling with them.

Like us, they were adopting for the first time. They happily enumerated the positive and challenging qualities they had seen in each of the three children. This family anticipated a rather rocky beginning, but they were committed to making it work. Because it was off-season for their seasonal business, both parents planned to spend the first six months at home to help everyone adjust to their new life together. Compared to what they were undertaking, our little venture seemed like nothing. The funny thing was how amazed they were by our plan to add an eighth child to our family. While we were all quite polite, I think each family thought the other was more than a little crazy.

PRACTICAL

While there are certainly reasons to space children within a family, the challenge of love is to embrace each child that God would send us. This openness to the creative will of the Holy Spirit is no less a part of adoption than it is of childbirth. Because adoption doesn't just "happen," it is a bit easier for us to sidestep the matter.

Many parents of both large and small families choose to adopt more than one child at a time. Often, bringing home a few children at once is the result of trying to keep a group of biological siblings together. In those instances, the process of adoption involves not just welcoming individual children, but a whole set of ready-made family relationships. The gifts of this kind of adoption are rich. Parents who seek children find them. Children who need parents receive them. And brothers and sisters, who may have been lost to one another, are secured together in one family.

There are plenty of other reasons for families to multiply rather than add when pursuing an adoption. Parents whose long-term plan includes more than one adopted child may find it easier to expand rather than repeat the process. While this may divide parental attention among the brood, children often bond to each other more quickly when they experience the adjustments they must make together. Whether a family adopts biological siblings or not, those who bring home more than one child at a time minimize both time and expense. This is especially true for those who adopt internationally.

Families who are considering adopting more than one child at a time should do their best to understand and assess the demands of parenting. That may be more difficult for couples who have not yet had children. Parents familiar with child-raising, however, should recognize that each child has unique needs, and no one parenting technique works for all. I found I needed a whole new set of mommy tools when we brought our adoptive daughter home.

Adopting a few children at one time may feel like creating an "instant family." But the single most important thing for any adoptive family to keep in mind is that the family God wants to build will take time. In reality, there is nothing instant about it. Being gentle with one another—and with ourselves—is essential to creating a happy and complete life together. Patience leads us to develop the generous and hospitable spirit that turns a house into a home and a collection of individuals into a loving family.

Think it through

❧ Have you thought about adopting more than one child now or at some time in the future?

❧ If you discover that the child you intend to adopt has a sibling who is also available for adoption, what will you do?

❧ Do you have a strategy for managing the relationships between children?

❧ Is there anything you might be able to do to help your family member or friend manage responsibilities during the first few months?

Pray it through

HOLY SPIRIT, SPIRIT OF ABUNDANCE, open our hearts wide enough to receive all that you long to give us. Fill our homes with life and love. Help us to welcome all the children you have planned for us. Touch us with your compassion, and give us the grace to respond with compassion to others. Make our lives fruitful and generous. Enable us to allow ourselves to become vulnerable to your inspirations. Teach us to build our family patiently. Help us to be gentle with others and with ourselves. Give us a spirit of hospitality. Guide us in adding new members to our family. Give hope to the children you will ask us to receive, and help them to receive us into their lives as well. Amen.

The Process

CHAPTER 12

Domestic and International Adoption

Love Seeks

Now the LORD said to Abram, "Go from your country and your kindred and your father's house to the land that I will show you."

— GENESIS 12:1

REFLECTION

When Abram first heard God's call, he may well have scratched his head in wonder. I can only imagine how Abram had to build up enough courage to talk to his wife, Sarai, about what he had heard. Told to leave everything behind, he was asked to pack up his whole life—family, friends, livelihood—and move. But where were they supposed to go?

That, in fact, was the most puzzling aspect of the whole business. The call to leave was very clear; their destination, however, was anything but. God was not simply asking them to pull up stakes and start over somewhere else. The Almighty was telling them to trust him completely and to trade the life they had made for themselves for one that he would give them.

Wanderers with no knowledge of where they were going or when and how they would get there, they must have wondered just how they were supposed to know when they had arrived. Certainly, there would be no one to greet them. They would find no sign carved into a cliff that said, "Welcome to Your New Home." We might be tempted to call this couple "directionless," but God called them "faithful."

PERSONAL

When we decided to adopt a child, it was immediately clear to us that our call was an international one. Our intention was to snatch a child from the worst set of prospects a child could face. We also did not want to take a child from prospective parents who, for reasons of their own, wished to adopt only from within the United States. Initially, we explored adopting from India, China, and Guatemala. One by one, all those doors closed.

After a few broken noses we learned that when doors slam in our faces, it is often God's way of telling us that they are simply the wrong doors. With further investigation, we began to see that Russia was the clear choice for us. One of the worst places on earth to be an orphan at the time, Russia had hundreds of thousands of homeless children. Of those who did grow up in the system, only twenty percent would go on to live relatively normal lives. The rest ended up either in prison or prostitution, on drugs—or dead. Those harsh realities drew us like moths to a flame.

Kara and John chose to adopt domestically. Because there are very few orphanages in the United States, domestic adoptions typically involve foster care or legal guardianship. Many adoptive parents have been a child's foster parents. That was not the situation in their case. The United States is also one of the few places in which adoption placement decisions are frequently made even before the child is born. Birth mothers exercise a high level of control over where their children are placed. Because of this, interaction with a child's birth mother at some level is a generally accepted part of the process. For John and Kara, this part of their experience became the most precious.

PRACTICAL

Adoptions in most foreign countries are "closed." Little or no information about birth parents may be given. On the other hand, no information about adoptive parents is accessible to birth parents. The paperwork for an international adoption is more involved than it is for a domestic adoption. The cost of travel can also be significant, and legal immigration and citizenship must be secured. Language barriers, too, play a significant role in the process and make medical information more difficult to decipher. Legal finalization is generally immediate and the waiting time relatively short. Many parents complete an adoption in less than a year. Ours took less than six months.

Most domestic adoptions are "open." Adoptive parents know a great deal about their son's or daughter's background, and the child is assured of access to all his or her birth and adoption records. The process allows for parents to adopt newborn babies, though the wait for referral and placement can be long. In most cases, a significant amount of time must pass before an adoption is finalized. The continued presence of biological parents or grandparents in the adopted child's life is a matter that is negotiated between birth and adoptive parents. Regular interaction can be rare, or not at all, or include a full set of visitation arrangements.

Any aspect of an adoption process can be considered a plus or a minus. For some, the thought of traveling halfway around the world to adopt is exciting. For others, it is terrifying. There are as many reasons to prefer open adoption as there are to choose a process that is closed. Looking at the options through the lens of your family's individual needs and perspective is the only way to see things clearly. Your own history or culture may draw you to a particular place. You may have a friend or relative who has adopted a child you have grown to love. Or you may know of a particular child who needs a home. No one path to adoptive parenthood is traveled by all—or even most.

Still, God does not tell us to move without showing us the way. He rarely, however, shows us the whole journey. God gives us only as much information as we actually need, rarely more, lest we stop trusting and following the lead of the Holy Spirit. Often, we are given only one step at a time—the next step we are meant to take. We may feel as if we are being called into the dark and distant unknown. The land that God will show us, however, is exactly that: the one that will be revealed to us as we go. That land may be far away or just around the corner.

Think it through

❧ Do you feel drawn to adopt from a particular place?

❧ Are you comfortable dealing with another country's legal system and process?

- Are there doors you believe that God is opening or closing?
- Do you think children adopted domestically are different from those who are adopted internationally?

Pray it through

HOLY SPIRIT, GUIDING LIGHT, show us clearly the land where you would have us go. Lead us along the pathways of your perfect will to the place that you have promised us. Whether near or far, at home or abroad, be always at our side. Give us the strength we need to finish the journey we begin. Protect us as we travel, and help us to be gracious guests. Keep us mindful of all those we leave behind. Give us the grace to find you wherever we are and to follow you rather than our own way. Bring us to the children you intend for us. Guide them and us safely home to one another and together to your eternal kingdom. Amen.

CHAPTER 13

The "Right" Agency

Love Advocates

"And I will ask the Father, and he will give you another Advocate..."

— JOHN 14:16

Likewise the Spirit helps us in our weakness; for we do not know how to pray as we ought, but that very Spirit intercedes with sighs too deep for words.

— ROMANS 8:26

REFLECTION

God never leaves us in the lurch—at least not for long. God helps us readily, not from a distance but from within our own hearts. This wonderful Spirit of God, alive in our souls, assists us even when we do not know how to ask for help; perhaps even when we do not know we need help. It is no coincidence that the Holy Spirit is called the Paraclete: the helper, comforter, intercessor, the one who is called to aid us. Jesus promised his disciples that they would have "another Advocate," because he knew that they would need one.

God rarely asks us to do things alone. Almost without exception, our callings are beyond us or, rather, beyond *just* us. The Holy Spirit's promptings usually require us to go outside of ourselves. While we easily acknowledge that living by faith means reaching out to others, we tend not to envision ourselves as needing assistance. Often, however, the most deeply spiritual times of our lives, the experiences that truly transform us, are those in which we are uncomfortably dependent on the help others are willing to give.

PERSONAL

Finding an adoption agency seemed a straightforward enough task, until my Internet search produced a list of over three million matches. Clicking through the first few pages, I couldn't imagine being able to choose an agency with any more assurance than if I had picked a name out of a hat. It seemed to both my husband and me that the process was more arbitrary and random than we had hoped. That realization was disconcerting.

While there were genuine differences between agencies, we were at a loss as to how to determine whether those variables were significant or not. Some agencies were large, others small. Some were strictly domestic, others specialized in one or more foreign countries. There were those that had a definite religious feel, and others that maintained a purely secular image. Costs also varied. There were agencies that seemed to advocate more strongly for the needs of the child, and others that emphasized the desires of the prospective parents. Some attempted a more balanced approach to family "matchmaking."

The task of choosing an agency felt like playing "Pin-the-tail-on-the-donkey." Blindfolded and dizzy, we asked God to put us into the right hands. There was no real way of making a decision with so many options and possibilities. In the end, I whittled the choices down to a short list of three.

After checking references and giving due diligence to the substantive differences between agencies, we made a choice by listening to our hearts: a small family-run agency in Oklahoma that specialized in adoptions from Russia. Although all our interaction in the United States was done by phone, e-mail, and snail mail, our agency fully understood our motivation to adopt and the perspective from which we pursued adoption. We were able to trust them not only to act for us, but with us.

Practical

Because adopting a child is a personal and lifelong journey, trusting the advice and expertise of others is not always easy. We all come to the adoption process with a purpose—and perhaps a calendar—in mind. That purpose often involves much more than simply bringing home a child. We all have hopes and dreams for our children, even for those who are not yet ours. We also have expectations of the process itself.

While most of what adoptive parents seek is reasonable, some things we hope for may not be completely realistic. Every family has areas in which its members can be flexible and those in which they dare not *be*. Our family knew that adopting a child with serious medical conditions would not be prudent. But what we didn't know until we met our daughter was that we didn't really *need* to adopt an infant. Age was something we could be flexible about. A good agency will assist prospective parents in the wise discernment of matters that arise over the course of the process.

Selecting an adoption agency is a choice that will affect almost every other aspect of your adoption journey. In essence, you are choosing a Sherpa to accompany you on the climb, a guide into territory where the air—and the ice—can be thin. And while it may not seem so at the time, you are selecting a particular process as well. In the end, most people choose an agency that feels right. Practical considerations are important, but not nearly as critical as being convinced that you are working with people whom you believe are worthy of your trust.

Ultimately, though, we can trust that the God who created families in the first place will continue to build them. Our heavenly Father is no less involved in adoption than he is in birth, and at times, more visibly so. Whatever connections you use to adopt, the Holy Spirit is your invisible adoption agent and facilitator, the unseen coordinator of the process you will undertake, and the power behind your ability to complete it.

Think it through

- Have you found an adoption agency you are comfortable working with?

- Do you trust that the people who are helping you to adopt a child are on your side?

- Has your agency helped you to clarify what you can and cannot be flexible about in adopting your child?

- Are there any warning signs you see in what your family members or friends have told you about their adoption agency?

Pray it through

HOLY SPIRIT, FRIEND OF SOULS, we place ourselves in your hands. Lead us to those who will help us. Empower us to trust in your care and in those who will make the journey with us. Work your will in every part of the process we are about to undertake. Teach us patience and perseverance. Give us confidence in your word to us, and in all the unseen aspects of our lives. O Paraclete, inspire us to advocate for others, to support and encourage them to follow the paths they take. Be our unfailing connection to heaven and to all our children. Even before we know who or where they are, bind us together in your love. Amen.

CHAPTER 14

Homestudy, Medicals, and Financials

Love Approves

Do your best to present yourself to God as one approved by him, a worker who has no need to be ashamed, rightly explaining the word of truth.

— 2 Timothy 2:15

If God is for us, who can be against us?

— Romans 8:31b

REFLECTION

In our culture of images and appearances, it may be helpful to remember that Shakespeare was wrong: the world is not really a stage on which life is "played"; nor are our relationships one long audition for a production in which some are given starring roles and others are stuck backstage operating the scenery and spotlights. We need not be too concerned with how our reviewers receive us, or even how we perceive our own "performance." Ultimately, God is our producer, director, and audience. The Lord's approval is the only one any of us really needs.

The Scriptures tell us to seek God as people already approved by him. Those who seek divine approval are empowered to do so because they already have it. Living our lives from a sense of being accepted by God changes everything. Suddenly, we have nothing to prove and no enemies to fear. We are free to forgive ourselves, free to laugh at ourselves, and free to give ourselves fully to the Lord and one another.

Faith is the answer to doubt, even to self-doubt. If we listen to our hearts, we may hear the inner dialogue between the voices of what we are and what we used to be, wish we were or hope to become. In the midst of that inner conversation, the Holy Spirit speaks a word of encouragement and freedom. That still, small voice assures us that we need not be concerned about how we measure up to others or even to our own standard of perfection. God wants us to be inspired by his ideals, not worried sick over them. Our heavenly Father is far more concerned with where we are headed than with where we are, and even less concerned with where we have been in the past. More than with us, God is *for* us.

PERSONAL

Seeking approval to adopt a child didn't bother me, but the idea of having a social worker come to our house did. I felt a tension that I hadn't perceived before—a tension between wanting to be good and feeling like I needed to *look* good. Anticipating some of the questions we might be asked, Andrew and I knew all we had to do was tell the truth. Somehow, that didn't seem as simple as it should have.

When I first spoke on the phone with Laura, our homestudy worker, I was extremely nervous. The truth is that after almost eighteen years of adult responsibility, I was afraid of not making the cut. I held my cards close to my chest, put on my best telephone voice (the one our kids laugh about), and made sure that there would be absolutely no interruptions. Laura seemed nice enough, but I really wasn't sure about how far to let my guard down. At the end of our conversation, I asked her if she saw herself as more of a gatekeeper or an advocate. When she answered "advocate," I stopped holding my breath, scheduled our home visit, and started cleaning.

When Laura arrived, she was every bit as positive in person as she had been on the phone. She didn't seem concerned about how clean everything was, nor did she seem to be looking for reasons to keep us from adopting. Gathering everyone together after her tour of the house and initial interview, Laura asked our kids about our plan to adopt. After fielding their rather excited responses, she simply said, "Let's do it!" Our interviews after that felt a lot more like conversation between friends.

PRACTICAL

Self-gift is the heart of adoption. Whenever we present ourselves, we make a present of ourselves. That is why a homestudy can be a bit unsettling—we're afraid that our "present" may be rejected as inadequate. Reasonable people recognize that it is necessary to assess prospective parents and their environments and protect the interests of adoptive children. Nevertheless, it is natural to feel anxious when you are the one being evaluated. There is no need to fear, however. Every family has its share of both shining virtues and glaring deficiencies. No family is perfect, not even those that look like they might be!

More than anything else, the homestudy establishes a professional support relationship that serves as an adoptive family's first link to resources they didn't even know existed. Laura, for example, was able to give us solid guidance regarding our daughter's development and bonding. Later, in post-placement visits, she provided a good reality check for our expectations.

The process of homestudy can be one of family self-discovery. Those who view it as just a necessary inconvenience—a bureaucratic hoop to jump through—will miss its real value. The information you will be required to provide can help you to identify and acknowledge both your strengths and weaknesses. Homestudy encompasses just about every aspect of life that could impact an adopted child: finances, job security, marital stability, medical issues, personal support systems, cultural awareness, prospective parents' own personal development, commitment to education, and attitudes toward adoption and parenting. Having all that data at hand can give you a clear picture of where you are. It can also provide the motivation to follow through on some of those things you've always meant to address.

Think it through

- How does the prospect of a homestudy make you feel?
- Do you find it easy to identify your family's strengths?
- Are there weaknesses in your family life that would benefit from some expertise or assistance?

❧ Is there something you can do to reassure your family member or friend during the application process?

Pray it through

HOLY SPIRIT, SEAL OF GOD on our hearts, give us the grace to let go of any fear or worries we may have. We trust that you have brought us to this path and will lead us on this journey. Help us to experience the depth of your unconditional love. O Comforter, give us the peace that comes from knowing you accept us, and teach us how to fully accept ourselves. Teach us how to make good use of both our strengths and weaknesses, and give us the humility to place all we are into your hands. Guide us to the resources we will need. Surround the child you intend for us with your loving presence. Amen.

CHAPTER 15

Open or Closed Adoption?

Love Respects

These are the words of the holy one, the true one,
who has the key of David,
who opens and no one will shut,
who shuts and no one opens:
    "I know your works. Look, I have set before you an open
    door, which no one is able to shut."

— Revelation 3:7b–8a

And no one in heaven or on earth or under the earth was able
to open the scroll or to look into it.

— Revelation 5:3

Reflection

The more we learn, the more we realize how little knowledge we
possess. Thankfully, in life we can and do experience more than

what we are able to fully comprehend. That is, while most of us *have* it, not many of us "get it!" Our relationship with God has this same quality. While we can know information about God, and even encounter the Lord in a personal way, the Eternal Being is far too mysterious for any of us to grasp completely. Ostriches and penguins have wings, but neither can fly. Likewise, we are limited by what we are.

It is astonishing that the God who has no limits never limits our access to his heart. Our heavenly Father is continuously available, forever open to us—even when we are not open to him. No one can close what God opens, and the Lord chooses to open himself to all. Further, no one can open what God closes. That is, no one can uncover what God does not reveal. God is the divine Revealer as well as the subject of divine revelation.

PERSONAL

"Open" adoption is understood to be an inclusive sharing of the child's family bonds between members of both birth and adoptive families. Not long after they brought their newborn son home, John and Kara shared their story with me. Their baby's birth mother was a college student who had been raised in an active Catholic family. Facing the difficult decisions of a crisis pregnancy, she was grateful to have found a practicing Catholic couple who were hoping to adopt a child. When the baby's arrival was near, Kara and John flew to the state where the baby's mom lived. Though she was young and scared, she invited them to be present when their son was born. Not long afterward, she placed her child in Kara's arms. Sobbing, the two women embraced. Each one thanked the other. Both were profoundly grateful.

"Closed" adoption is understood to be an exclusive transfer of the child's family bonds to his or her adoptive family. When my husband and I decided to adopt, we knew that whatever approach we took would affect not only the child we brought home, but also the children already at home. Our calling was to extend the family we had built by making an adoptive child part of it. We envisioned all our children—biological and adoptive—sharing the same set of relationships. The last thing we wanted was a radical change in family life for the seven kids we already had. For us, incorporating members of an adopted child's birth family into our established family life just wasn't a viable, or desirable, choice.

Practical

Adoption is a profoundly personal matter that involves the private lives of a number of people. As one might expect, there are numerous viewpoints about how to handle sensitive information in a respectful manner. The debate between those who advocate agreements at the opposite poles of the adoption spectrum does not provide much assistance to prospective parents. What parents need to know is that there is no single best or right way to adopt a child. Almost any arrangement can work well, if boundaries regarding privacy are mutually accepted and respectfully maintained.

Every form of adoption offers the child a particular set of advantages. Closed adoption gives everyone involved the stability that comes from clearly defined family relationships. Those who champion closed adoption often express concern that children who grow up with two sets of parents may experience a sense of divided loyalty or confusion. Those who advocate open adoption believe that keeping a child personally connected to his own history is an advantage. Their hope is that by maintaining relationships where possible, families may be more equipped to address the questions of identity that are often intensified for the adopted child.

It is equally true that issues arise from all types of adoption arrangements. Parents who choose a closed adoption believing that this will functionally eliminate the need to deal with a child's birth parents will find that they are mistaken. Every adopted child lives with the consequences, both positive and negative, of his or her family relationships, even if the relationships are not ongoing. Parents who opt to include birth relatives in their child's upbringing may discover that agreements made are not always kept. Some families have struggled with limiting those who seek more than the agreed-upon amount of personal contact with a child. Others have had to explain to their adoptive child why a birth parent has chosen to drop out of their lives. Adoptive parents may also find themselves less than enthused about the influence a birth parent may have on their child's moral and spiritual development.

It is difficult to evaluate what kind of adoption is best for children. Even when everyone involved focuses on the long-term interests of the child, determining and implementing what is best is not always possible. The most important thing you can do is think through what you can live with and what you are willing to welcome into your family life. It helps to realize that each child and every adoption is unique. There is no "one-size-fits-all" adoption arrangement.

Think it through

➤ Would you be comfortable with facilitating an ongoing relationship between your adoptive child and his/her birth parents?

❧ How will you help your child understand and accept that there are things none of you will ever be able to know about his or her birth family?

❧ Are you able to seek legal advice from a competent professional?

❧ Are you able to help your friend or family member discern what kind of adoption is right for them without passing judgment or voicing your preferences too strongly?

Pray it through

HOLY SPIRIT, WISE COUNSELOR, give us a clear understanding of the doors we have chosen to open and those that we have shut. Give us the grace to enter through the gate that you have chosen for us. Help us know what to expect and to be content in the process we pursue. Teach us to recognize hidden gifts, and sustain us in times of question or doubt. Empower us to be faithful to our commitments and to find in that faithfulness a source of joy. Guide us always forward in your will. Build our family in a way that will serve you well. Open our hearts to the children you will give us, and open their hearts to the love you have inspired for them in our hearts. Amen.

CHAPTER 16

The Paper Pregnancy

Love Labors

If every one of them were written down, I suppose that the world itself could not contain the books that would be written.

— JOHN 21:25B

Those who conquer will inherit these things, and I will be their God and they will be my children.

— REVELATION 21:7

REFLECTION

Jesus lived a relatively short life on earth. So much happened during the three years of his public ministry, however, that John ends his Gospel by telling us that not even all the libraries in all the world could hold what it would take to record everything Jesus did.

There is more to everything than anyone can learn from reading a book. Even those who read all that has been written on a subject do not end up knowing all there is to know. Life is bigger than what we can fit onto a page, or even thousands of pages. Paper and life are not well matched, for while the page begins empty, our lives start off filled beyond the margins.

This is even truer when it comes to people. We struggle to put our experiences into words, and find it nearly impossible to express who we are on paper. We hope that what we communicate is a window into our hearts. But as we go deeper, we cannot help but wonder whether our inner beings have a lot less to do with what is at the surface than we once thought. People are far more than any documentation their lives can produce. Sometimes, they are profoundly different from what can be written about them.

Personal

Biological parents float along their way with very little paperwork. Adoptive parents find themselves swimming in it. When the thick envelope of blank forms to fill out came from our agency, I was delighted. Looking at the document checklist, I felt like a racehorse just released from the gate, ready to run hard to the finish. I wanted it all done yesterday. The volume of what was required, however, forced me to take a slower pace.

With so many people to contact, annoying little obstacles to overcome, and details to keep track of, I had to find a sensible rhythm to the process. We were able to make steady progress when we stopped looking at the whole of what had to be done, and started taking it one piece at a time. The key was to do something every day, rather than trying to do everything at once. We stuck with it even when it felt as if we were chipping away at Mount

Everest with an ice pick. Our paperwork was complete in about two months.

PRACTICAL

The sheer volume of information that must be gathered and submitted is substantial. Among the requirements: marriage license, medical information, financial data, criminal records, deeds to property, letters of recommendation, personal statements, all individually notarized.

For those adopting internationally, there are the added joys of immigration clearance, citizenship applications, and an official fingerprinting of all adults living in the household. It was a bit strange to take my then eighty-seven-year-old grandmother for fingerprinting—even stranger when she told the government official it was for an international adoption! All submitted information is then translated. In addition to notarization, each separate document going overseas must also receive a special seal. *Apostilles* are obtained from the state in which the document originated. If you were born in Ohio, married in Iowa, and now live in Texas . . .

The mass of paper that results from all this flurry—properly collated, of course—is the dossier. Getting it done can be rather stressful. Dotting every "i" and crossing every "t" is a monumental and lengthy process. Those who make the mistake of thinking that adoption is somehow less involved than biological childbearing soon find that pregnancy has a paper equivalent.

It is easy to get caught up in the excitement of adopting a child, and almost as easy to get tripped up by the intricacies involved. Parents who recognize that adoption has its own process and timetable are already ahead of the game. Those who try to exercise control are likely to experience a great deal of unnecessary frustration and anxiety. It is wiser to give yourself over to the process than it is to fight it. Swimming frantically against the current does not result in a faster adoption or a "better" child. On the other hand, a prospective parent who procrastinates will not be able to accomplish what needs to be done. Setting realistic goals and deadlines will help you complete what you need to do. As you begin wading through the paperwork the end will not be in sight. But there is an end to the process you are pursuing.

Those who stay the course finish it in time, if not on time. You may not know how long the road is, but the one you are traveling will lead you to a child. Love perseveres. What it takes to assemble your dossier is just a taste of the persistent love that will come to permeate your family life. It is the love that conquers, the love by which we become the children of God.

Think it through

⚜ Do you consider yourself or your spouse administratively skilled or organizationally challenged?

⚜ Can you be gentle with yourself in assembling the documents you will need?

⚜ Are you committed to representing yourselves honestly?

⚜ Is there any practical assistance or tool you can offer to your friend or family member to help them persevere through the process?

Pray it through

HOLY SPIRIT, SPIRIT OF PERSEVERANCE, help us to do what must be done. Protect us from anxiety and doubt. Keep our eyes on what lies beyond the task, and guide us through each step with diligence. Guard our hearts from the desire to control. Defend our souls from discouragement. Comfort us when we are tired and overwhelmed. Gently show us the truth about ourselves, and give us the grace to tell that truth without fear. Help us to finish what has been set before us. Watch over our children as we do what is necessary to bring them home. Amen.

CHAPTER 17

The Waiting Parent

Love Is Patient

Now hope that is seen is not hope, for who hopes for what is seen? But if we hope for what we do not see, we wait for it with patience.

— ROMANS 8:24–25

"Do not let your hearts be troubled. Believe in God, believe also in me. In my father's house there are many dwelling places. If it were not so, would I have told you that I go to prepare a place for you? And if I go and prepare a place for you, I will come again and will take you to myself, so that where I am, there you may be also."

— JOHN 14:1–3

Reflection

Nothing is more difficult than waiting. Whether we anticipate the future with joy or dread, there is something deep in human nature that resists—even resents—having to wait. We find the interim an intolerable place to be. The world we live in is not exactly conducive to patience. Express lines, text messages, high-speed internet: it's amazing how five seconds can feel like forever. Even though we can get what we want faster than ever, we find it increasingly difficult to remain hopeful. In truth, patience and hope are related. If one is missing, chances are that the other will not be found either.

We tend to talk about hope as if it were some kind of vain wish. We hope for good weather. We hope the waitress comes to take our order soon. We hope that our team wins the game. The Scriptures paint a very different picture. Hope is not something we wish for. Hope is something we expectantly wait for. When we wish, it is because we cannot bring about whatever we are wishing for. Hope, however, belongs to those who have done everything they can do. Hope is not passive. It is the act of trusting God to bring about what we desire according to the divine will.

When we trust, we are able to wait patiently. Knowing that something good will come, we are content to have something to look forward to. Patience is the fruit of that conviction. It rises with hope in the hearts of those who believe what they do not see. Impatience, on the other hand, is rooted in the desire to control. Those who find it difficult to trust that things will turn out for the best tend toward panic. Often rushing into the middle of a situation, they intervene more from desperation than from vision. In the end, they may not even realize that all they ever really needed to do was wait.

Personal

Things should have settled down when all of our paperwork was done, but they didn't simply because I couldn't. For some reason, no longer having a stack of things to do made me nervous and compulsive. I became anxious about almost everything to do with our plan to adopt. Questions flooded my mind all day long, and even kept me up at night. *When were we going to hear something? Where would we be sent? What would we find when we got there? Were we doing the right thing?* Impatience grew as I allowed myself to be consumed by the desire to *know*. All that inner churning, however, prevented me from making genuine preparations. The waiting could have been joyful. Instead, it was aggravating.

Practical

Adoptions have no due date. Strangely, though, there seems to be a clock that starts ticking inside us as soon as we initiate the process to adopt. Taking each step as it comes, there are times when everything seems to move at the speed of light. There are also quiet periods lasting weeks or even months, times when it appears that nothing is happening. The flurry of activity may overwhelm us. The quiet, however, challenges us to accept the fact that we are not in control.

Holding patiently onto hope is not as simple as it sounds. People who have waited several years to have a child often fear yet another disappointment. Others may not fully appreciate the twists and turns inherent in the adoption process. Ultimately, however, we must come to the point of making a decision to trust the Spirit who first prompted us to complete what he started. We are able to do so when we can place our time into the context of God's eternity.

While we may not feel that waiting furthers the adoption process, in truth, it serves the adopting family well. Waiting gives you time for real preparation. It is a sabbatical for both learning and rest. Having few active items on your to-do list provides an opportunity to reflect and to plan. The time you spend waiting can be profitable if you make good use of it. Rooms can be set up. Schools can be contacted. Advice can be sought out. All the necessary parental accessories can be purchased—and assembled. Even more, you will have the luxury of being able to sort through all that you are feeling. Rest, reflect, and enjoy one another while you are still able to do so freely. Once your child arrives home, you may have far less time for those things than you might expect.

God is always preparing us. There is not a day that goes by or a lesson we have learned that God will not eventually use for our benefit. Those piano lessons you took as a child, the time you helped your father fix the shingles on the roof, the demanding eighth grade English teacher nobody liked, the loser you are embarrassed to admit you ever dated—every experience of our lives can be a divine preparation. The heavenly Father is ever working in each one of us, making us ready to receive him and one another. The deepest preparations are those made in the heart. God does not plant seeds in untilled soil.

Think it through

- Is there something you have done or experienced that you can now see as part of how God prepared you to adopt a child?

- Can you think of a situation in which you felt truly hopeful?

- What makes waiting easier for you?

- Is there something you can do today to help your family member or friend remain hopeful?

Pray it through

HOLY SPIRIT, SPIRIT OF PATIENCE AND PEACE, teach us how to
wait joyfully in hope. Calm our hearts and minds. Keep us from
frenzy and guard us from apathy. Help us to rest in confidence and
to be grateful for the time you have given us to prepare our homes.
Show us how to make the deeper preparations, to ready our hearts—
and not just our houses—to receive the children you will give us.
Inspire us to trust you and to entrust ourselves and our children to
your care. Fill our days and nights with your peace. And lead us all
to the place you are preparing for us to dwell with you forever.
Amen.

CHAPTER 18

Lost Referrals

Love Is Vulnerable

Can a woman forget her nursing child,
or show no compassion for the child of her womb?
Even these may forget,
yet I will not forget you.
See, I have inscribed you on the palms of my hands . . .

— Isaiah 49:15–16

REFLECTION

Though the world is full of people, God does not forget any of us. We may be forgotten by everyone: friends, neighbors, colleagues, relatives, even our own mothers. Not one of us, however, is lost to the eternal heart of God. We are etched into the palm of the Father's hand by love, whether returned or unrequited. There, we are held forever.

PERSONAL

Early in our adoption process, we were informed that Russian law gave preference to Russian families and that foreigners were viewed as a last resort for children who needed homes. On our final day in Yulia's city, our adoption facilitator cautioned that, until our adoption was finalized, we could lose her if a Russian family expressed interest in adopting her. He asked how quickly we could return to Russia for a court date and advised us to move full-steam ahead through the process in order to reduce the possibility of losing the little girl we already had begun to think of as our daughter. We decided to shoot for a court date only three weeks later.

We hadn't even left Russia and were already setting up the logistics for our return. As we parted, the facilitator handed us a few additional forms (yes, more paperwork!) that we would need to complete in the short time at home. These identified Yulia as the child we were going to adopt. It was wonderful to see her name next to ours instead of a blank line.

We left Russia a few days later with a great deal of excitement and a few clouds of apprehension. I remember thinking on the plane home how horrifying it would be to lose our little girl. It was hard to imagine taking a different child home as our daughter. Anyone else would seem like an impostor. I wondered if I could even continue with an adoption if Yulia's smiling face wouldn't be waiting at the end of it all. This after having met her only a few days before and spending a grand total of about six hours together!

PRACTICAL

There is a mysterious force that draws us to certain children. Sometimes it operates through a photograph, or a story, or a name.

Although Andrew and I didn't feel an inner pull to take home every child we met, there was another child who captured my heart. Olga was one of the little girls who had walked into the room with our daughter when we first met her. Even smaller than Yulia, Olga was frail and cautious with strangers. The entire time she was in the room with us, she sat on the lap of one of the orphanage caregivers. A sweet child, Olga was obviously delighted by the little barrettes the orphanage workers had placed in her pale blonde curls. Even though I knew she was not meant for us, I prayed that Olga would find a family and that God would bless her with a new life of hope. For months after I got home, I thought about her. From time to time, after many years, I still do.

Adopting parents do occasionally lose a child they intend to adopt to a birth mother, the child's relatives, or even another adoptive family. The grief of losing an adoption referral can feel a lot like suffering a miscarriage—even when the best interests of the child are assured. Prospective parents dealing with a lost referral feel angry and untrusting. Suddenly, and perhaps for reasons that may be difficult to accept, joyful expectation gives way to disappointment.

The anguish of such a loss is very real. For couples that have struggled with infertility, that pain may be intensified by its familiarity. Well-intentioned friends and family may expect everyone to take it all in stride, but prospective parents who lose a referral will need time to heal. Families should go gently, however, giving themselves adequate time to grieve before reentering the process. Parents who have lost a referral observe that, even after successfully adopting another child, they remain emotionally attached to the child they "lost."

Moving on with hope is both desirable and possible. Ultimately, the pain of remembering our loss is far sweeter than the comfort we may find in forgetfulness. Faith teaches us that no human encounter is wasted. Every time we meet another person, we meet the One who created us all. Perhaps the child you thought was yours was meant to be someone else's all along. But the love you found in that little face, the joy you felt at the sound of that name, the plans and hopes and dreams you grasped for a time were given to you for a lasting purpose.

In the midst of the uncertainties we face, it is comforting to know that a family seeking to adopt is likely to bring a child home. The path toward adoption has its share of twists and turns—some more painful than others. The challenge throughout is one of trust. Many prospective parents experience moments when it is hard to keep believing in their adoption dream. Those times, however, provide an opportunity for us to place our trust where it truly belongs: in the Holy Spirit who inspired us to adopt in the first place. Parents who do so will discover that the Spirit God sends to inspire also guides and comforts us. That very same Holy Spirit consoles and heals us when things don't go the way we expect or hope.

Think it through

- How much control do you think you have over your adoption process? Is it enough for you?

- What could enable you to trust that the child you eventually adopt is the child God had planned for your family all along?

- Do you have any unresolved grief over losses you have suffered in the past?

- How would you bring comfort to your friend or family member if something disrupted their adoption process in some way?

Pray it through

HOLY SPIRIT, SPIRIT OF SOLACE AND CONSOLATION, we thank you for your gifts, even if they are only for a time. Give us the grace to surrender every aspect of our lives to your perfect will. Help us to accept losses without anger or despair. Show us how to grieve in your presence. Nurture hope in our hearts and faith-filled trust in our souls. Teach us to remember with sweetness those children who were almost ours. Keep us from losing the gift of love they brought into our lives. Enable us to release them to the love of others. We ask you to give them the families they need and deserve. Remember them, as we do, and bless them. Amen.

CHAPTER 19

Getting the Call

Love Rejoices

But when the fullness of time had come, God sent his Son born of a woman, born under the law, in order to redeem those who were under the law, so that we might receive adoption as children. And because you are children, God has sent the Spirit of his son into our hearts, crying "Abba! Father!" So you are no longer a slave, but a child, and if a child then also an heir, through God.

— GALATIANS 4:4–7

REFLECTION

Life is not a stream of random events punctuated by a few coincidences. Looking back, every one of us can see emerging patterns and themes in events that were not apparent to us at the time.

Characters come and go. They themselves evolve and all the while they transform us. Events, both positive and negative, shape us by how we respond to them. In turn, our actions influence the lives of others.

We have all witnessed instances in which events are mysteriously drawn together and things fall into place. That is the essence of what the Scriptures call "the fullness of time." Time rarely reaches its fullness when we expect or want it to. But when the moment arrives, there is nothing that we can do to stop or delay it. God moves when we have finished taking our turn. When he does, however, it often feels as if we are suddenly playing a different game.

Faith teaches us that God is personally involved in human affairs. God is not merely our Creator, but also our Father. Our lives have a purpose and a goal. The divine will works in, through, and around us to bring about the fullness of who we are and why we are. We do not need to wonder if we are in the right place at the right time. If we are in God's hands, we are never anywhere else.

Personal

At some point during our adoption process, it occurred to me that timing was the single most influential factor in determining which child would ultimately become ours. In our family's case, that turned out to be true in spades. The child we adopted was almost completely determined by when we were told to book our trip.

We had hoped to travel during a week of winter school vacation, but as things progressed, it did not seem that would work out. Suddenly, however, all the necessary pieces lined up. Our paperwork had made it overseas, and we were able to book the first of our two trips to Russia in February, as we had hoped. Our call to fly came suddenly.

While I was thrilled by the prospect of finding our daughter, I admit to feeling a bit apprehensive about how quickly things seemed to be moving. No one wanted to run through the process faster than I. But when the call came, I had the inner sense of being rushed. It was not until much later on that we realized why everything had to move as quickly as it did.

During that first trip, we met a number of children; one of them was our daughter. Later on we were told that if we had traveled three months later, our little girl would not have been at the orphanage we had visited. Around the time of her third birthday in May, she would have been moved out of the "baby house" to a facility for older children. Because we had requested an infant, we would never have met her. Similarly, if we had decided to adopt a year earlier, we would not have been sent to our daughter's region. Her city had been legally closed to international adoption for a period of nearly two years. Either earlier or later and we would have adopted a different child. Our daughter would not have become ours.

Practical

In the adoption process, once all the paperwork is done, the next step is ordinarily the referral. We traveled "blind" to find our own "referral." Usually, however, an agency calls when an individual child has been matched to prospective parents by those who are responsible for the child's care. In other situations, the child available for adoption may not yet have been born. Adoptive parents may be asked to meet an expectant birth mother. Then too, there are parents who receive an emergency call from a local department of child services. However it is that the match is made, both prospective and birth parents have decisions to make—decisions that have suddenly become both specific and personal.

Every adopting parent runs to the phone when it rings, hoping to receive that long-awaited call from the adoption agency. But when that call does come, it is normal to feel a bit uncertain about what you are undertaking. Climbing the mountain of paperwork and preparations is arduous; reaching the peak is exhilarating. But when the ball starts rolling down the hill, most adoptive parents find they aren't nearly as ready as they thought they were.

You may have waited for years, months, or weeks to hear the news that you would soon meet your new son or daughter. Likely, you will have had all your ducks in a row well in advance of receiving that much anticipated phone call. All you will need to do when the phone rings is answer it. Go gently forward. No one will force you to take a step you do not feel good about. No child is ever adopted accidentally. You will have time to rediscover the love that first set you on the path to adoption—not less time than you need, but probably not more.

The Holy Spirit works precisely on schedule. Nobody has a better sense of timing than the Eternal One. God will bring together everything that is necessary just when it is necessary. When all the relevant people are in their proper places, just remember to hang on! Your hat may fly off your head; your stomach may feel a bit queasy; you might even let out a scream as you plunge into the thrill and adventure of family life. But oh, what a joyous ride it is!

Think it through

- Are you truly ready to receive the call you have anticipated and prayed for?
- Are you able to thoughtfully consider the referral that is made, or will your emotions make that difficult?
- Are you comfortable with the pace of what is happening?

❧ What can you do to help your family member or friend celebrate the good news?

Pray it through

HOLY SPIRIT, FINGER OF GOD, help us to see your presence in the process and to trust that things will unfold according to your will. Maker of divine appointments, bring us to the right place at the right time. Give us the grace to wait for the fullness of time and the wisdom to recognize that moment when it comes. Teach us to place our lives in your hands. Prepare us to receive what we have asked for. Prepare our children to receive us too. Give them hope and the reassurance of your embrace until that day when we share your warmth together. Amen.

CHAPTER 20

A Day in Court

Love Seals

"When they bring you before the synagogues, the rulers and the authorities, do not worry about how you are to defend yourselves, or what you are to say; for the Holy Spirit will teach you at that very hour what you ought to say."

— LUKE 12:11

So then, you are no longer strangers and aliens, but you are citizens with the saints and also members of the household of God . . .

— EPHESIANS 2:19

REFLECTION

The Spirit that inspires us also teaches us. God promises, in fact, that when we need the right words, we will find that he has placed them on our tongues. When we are brought before authorities of any kind, we need not worry about how we will acquit ourselves. The Holy Spirit will teach us what to do, and God will empower us to do or say what is necessary.

Like the judges in adoption courts, God creates families out of strangers. The child you will call your own, the one you will love for a lifetime and beyond, was once completely unknown to you. Foreigners, aliens with no connection to one another, by God's grace we all become members of one heavenly household. There is nothing for us to fear, for our judge is also our Father.

PERSONAL

We arrived in the city of Voronezh early on a Sunday morning, and we spent time visiting Yulia and preparing for our appearance in a Russian court the following day. Our facilitator told us that the judge would probably ask a few questions. Arriving at the court, we were introduced to the attorney who would represent us, a young man who seemed pleased with the kind of work he was doing. Our translator accompanied us into the courtroom where we saw one of the orphanage caregivers and an official from the region's Ministry of Education. The adoption facilitator stayed outside.

The room itself was small and in terrible disrepair. As I wondered if anything really official could happen there, the judge walked in. An older man sure of his authority, he came across as a bit gruff and more than a bit intimidating. We sat down, and the proceedings began.

The facts of Yulia's history and her medical prognosis were read aloud, and representatives from the government and the orphanage gave their statements in turn. Mostly, they emphasized how dim Yulia's future appeared and exaggerated any developmental issues she might have in order to give the judge even more reason to approve our adoption and waive the usual ten-day waiting period. It took less than two minutes for our attorney to present a summary of the mountain of paperwork we had been required to submit.

The judge thumbed through our dossier. Then he asked the question we had rehearsed the day before with our facilitator: "Why would anyone with seven children want to adopt another one?" Andrew stood up and talked about how much he loved children, how they were the light of his life, how he could not imagine living without them. The judge seemed unimpressed. Then it was my turn. Taking a different tack, I spoke about how we viewed adoption as being about not just what we could give to a child who needs a family, but also what that child would bring to us. Adopting Yulia, I said, was a way to teach our children generosity of heart and to experience how family is made by love that crosses every boundary, even birth, language, and culture. I'm not sure the judge appreciated what I said, but he was satisfied (or perplexed) enough to move on to question number two.

The second question was a lot easier to answer. "Why did you come to Russia instead of going somewhere else?" Reading the Slavic sounding names of our other children aloud, he asked if we had adopted the rest of our kids from Russia as well. When we told him they were all biological, he shook his head and stood up to leave the room. Twenty minutes later, the judge returned and announced that Yulia was now our daughter, Juliana.

A year and a half later, we re-adopted our daughter under the laws of the state we live in, a procedure necessary in order to obtain a U.S. birth certificate. The contrast between our two courthouse experiences couldn't have been greater. Calling our day in court "adoption day," we decided to make it a joyous occasion. Our whole family, grandparents, godparents, and even a priest friend were all welcomed into the judge's chambers, where a casual conversation about our adoption journey took place. The judge signed the adoption decree without asking much of anything. We shared the traditional Russian welcome of serving bread and salt and took a few photos. The priest performed the "Order for the Blessing of Parents and an Adopted Child," from the *Book of Blessings*, in the courthouse atrium.

Practical

Courtrooms and legal proceedings make everyone nervous, but there is no way to avoid the fact that adoption is, by its very nature, a legal proceeding. Every state and country has its own legal traditions and process. At times what is going on can be confusing and hard to understand. Whether the court is American or not, legalese in any place is a foreign language.

Our obligations under the law and the number of procedures we must follow are serious business. There is no substitute for good legal advice, and it is important for adopting families to fully understand the obligations they are expected to fulfill. These can include sending periodic updates to adoption regulators, court officials, and birth parents about how the child is progressing.

For many of us, the presence of judges, lawyers, and stenographers create a level of anxiety that clouds the love that motivates us to adopt. These, however, are precisely the people who make adoption possible, and help to keep it safe. While we may not be able to anticipate every question we will be asked, all we need to do is answer.

Think it through

➤ Do you know what protections the law affords you as well as what the law requires of you?

❧ Are you likely to feel intimidated or nervous in court? Is there something you can do in advance that can make you more confident?

❧ Is there something you can do to express your gratitude to those who have made adoption possible for you and your child?

❧ Are you able to accompany your friend or family member to court or send some other sign of your support?

Pray it through

HOLY SPIRIT, DIVINE TEACHER, place in our mouths the words we need. Give us courage before those who will judge us. Empower us to answer what is asked of us with confidence and truth. Protect us from nervousness and confusion. Inspire in us a respect for authority and law. Bless the judge before whom we will appear, and the lawyers and courtroom workers. Help them to appreciate the importance of what they do for families. Help us all to seek your will and to see your work to completion. Teach us, in all things, to trust in you without fear. Amen.

Your Child

CHAPTER 21

Meeting Your Child

Love Knows

Arise my love, my fair one, come away. . . .
[L]et me see your face,
let me hear your voice;
for your voice is sweet
and your face is lovely.

— Song of Solomon 2:13b; 14b

Reflection

We can't genuinely love each other at first sight. Our heavenly Father, however, manages to love us even *before* first sight. Each of us is the result of that love. We exist simply because God loves us into being.

The Lord's love for us does not grow. It begins in fullness and is a flower that never fades. While our love for the Holy One can wax and wane, the divine love we enjoy is ever constant. The Creator knows everything about his creation. There is nothing that our Father needs to discover about us. All things are seen by heaven's eyes.

In God's eyes every one of us is "fair and lovely." Our Father's great desire is to see the faces formed by his own hands and to hear the voices he gave us raised in song. The Holy Spirit invites each of us to arise and come. God leaves no one uninvited. The eternal wedding supper of the lamb is meant to gather all people as guests of the Most High.

PERSONAL

Yulia was the first child we met. Entering the room with two other little girls, she had us mesmerized from the moment we saw her. At the orphanage director's instruction, she sat down, stood up, greeted us, did a little dance, and stretched her red and black velour dress out to twirl. Exceptionally small for her age, it was hard to believe that she was almost three years old.

A child psychologist was brought in to explain Yulia's background. The psychologist commented that Yulia was considered a social child, playing well with other children. Evidently, she had a mind of her own too, and refused to eat foods she didn't like. That was quite an assertion of self for an orphan who did not have enough food to begin with!

Yulia responded with delight to every ounce of attention we gave her. When we showed her a family photo album we had brought along, she attempted to learn all the names of the strangers she saw inside. Affectionate and energetic, she was happy to try anything we suggested—even English.

We felt an instant connection to Yulia from the start. We felt drawn to her, attracted by everything we saw in her tiny but irresistible self. It was a force neither of us expected to encounter, certainly one far more formidable than any we had anticipated. We still can't quite figure out how such a skinny little wisp of a girl could have wielded such power!

While I was completely head-over-heels infatuated with Yulia, I can't say I genuinely loved her in those first moments, or days, or even weeks. This little girl speaking Russian baby talk, trapped on the other side of the world, needed us. It felt good to be needed like that.

It was easy to love the *idea* of loving Yulia, and we committed our lives to that idea. But I remember wondering if I could grow to love Yulia the way I loved our other children. I wondered because I knew that I didn't—at least not yet. In time, I discovered it *was* possible to love her that way, because I did.

PRACTICAL

Thousands of families claim to have loved their adopted children at first sight. Somehow, I think that "love" may be overstating things a bit. We can certainly perceive a personal chemistry or connection. We may also be deeply drawn to a particular child. Real love, however, both gives and takes much more than that.

It is unreasonable to expect that every photo, video, or first meeting with a child will fill every adoptive parent with a rush of spontaneous or overwhelming love. Many parents do not experience a special attraction to the child they expect to adopt. Some feel more estranged than connected. The truth is that few of us find every child equally attractive. In fact, we are bound to meet up with some children who—like some adults—turn us off. We may not even be able to pinpoint the reasons why.

First meetings may be difficult for family members who experience little or no emotion toward a child referred to them for adoption. Waiting to be hit by a romantic ton of bricks, parents may find themselves tempted to turn down a referral simply because the child does not evoke in them a strong emotional response.

Love, however, does not depend on how—or even if—we feel. The truth is that parents fall in and out of love with their children just as they fall in and out of love with each other. There are days of sweetness and affection, to be sure. But there are also seasons of annoyance and frustration.

Infatuation is not the stuff of parenting, commitment is. Adopting a child is not like shopping in a department store. People, after all, are not made to order. Ultimately, love is an act of will—a conscious and deliberate decision to devote ourselves to what is good for another. Because love is so much more than a feeling, it can grow despite any lack of feeling we may have. When we choose to love, we choose to grow in that love. We do not start out in full bloom. Adoption is a sprout from which the fragrant flowers of love may bud and blossom in time.

Think it through

* What do you expect to feel when you meet your child for the first time? What if your emotions don't line up with your expectations?

* What do you think your child will feel when he or she meets you for the first time?

* How can you strengthen your decision to love your child even before you meet him or her?

❧ Is there something you can do to help your family members or friends sort out their emotions?

Pray it through

HOLY SPIRIT, SPIRIT OF JOY, speak to our hearts. Keep our hearts open to all the children we meet. Guide us in interpreting what we see. Lead us to the children you have promised us. Give us wisdom to discern the information we receive. Help us to balance our expectations with the realities we encounter. Fill us with confidence in the choices we make, and teach us to walk by faith with joy. Help us to know your will for us and for the children with whom we will share life. Comfort any fears our children may have. Bless them with the same joy you have given us. Amen.

CHAPTER 22

Medical Mysteries

Love Trusts

But just when [Joseph] had resolved to do this, an angel of the Lord appeared to him in a dream and said, "Joseph, son of David, do not be afraid to take Mary as your wife, for the child conceived in her is from the Holy Spirit. She will bear a son, and you are to name him Jesus, for he will save his people from their sins." All this took place to fulfill what had been spoken by the Lord through the prophet:

"Look, the virgin shall conceive and bear a son,
and they shall name him Emmanuel,"
which means, "God is with us."

When Joseph awoke from sleep, he did as the angel of the Lord commanded him; he took her as his wife . . .

— MATTHEW 1:20–24

REFLECTION

Fear is a natural response to uncertainty. Even Joseph was afraid to fully commit himself to Mary and her child. That is why, in the midst of his restless nights, the Lord sent an angel to reassure Joseph with a dream. Telling him that Mary's child was conceived by the power of the Holy Spirit, the angel called Joseph from fear to faith. Love always brings forth trust in the face of anxiety. Joseph took Mary into his house because he was convinced that this was God's plan not only for her, but also for himself.

It is wonderful to realize that the Holy Family was both biological and adoptive. Mary gave birth to Jesus, and Joseph adopted him. Neither one of them fully understood what would be required of them as parents of the Son of God, nor could they comprehend the depth of God's gift to us all in Christ.

PERSONAL

As soon as we expressed interest in the possibility of adopting Yulia, we were led into the director's office where we listened as Yulia's medical files were read aloud. Because her entry into the world had not been officially recorded until her orphanage placement, very little was known about Yulia's birth. Her birth mother's name did not appear on the government registry of alcoholics or drug addicts. Nonetheless, after the state took custody of her, Yulia spent some time in the hospital for medical evaluation. She was diagnosed—as almost every Russian orphan is—with "residual perinatal encephalopathy." This shocking terminology, we later learned, described a condition entirely unfamiliar to American doctors and is applied with little or no substantiation. Her Russian lab tests for HIV, hepatitis, and other communicable diseases were all clear.

Developmental milestones were also recorded. Yulia sat up at about ten months and did not walk until she was fifteen months old. She was allegedly toilet-trained (more accurately, toilet-timed). At thirty-four months, Yulia was just beginning to talk (in Russian, of course!). She didn't catch cold often, but the files noted a "breath-holding incident"—whatever that was. She had fallen down once and been hospitalized with stitches on her forehead. Nothing was said about how very small Yulia was, except that she weighed twenty-two pounds, and was only thirty-one inches tall.

There was something very unsettling about hearing information which, in some sense, was none of our business. What struck me most was how much more information I had tucked into my brain about our other children's early years. Though the folder held everything that could be told about Yulia, it didn't take long to read. Clearly, whatever the orphanage director could tell us about Yulia's health and medical history would be just a few pieces of a vastly larger puzzle.

PRACTICAL

Fear about a child's medical history can cripple parents seeking to adopt. Often, there is an impulse to confirm and reconfirm; to get as many medical opinions and reviews as possible. Serious health issues may merit that kind of attention. But when it comes to more general concerns, there really is no way to know every detail of our adoptive children's health or medical history. No matter how diligent we are in seeking information, some relevant facts are bound to be left out.

Those unknowns, however, are also present for families with biological children. Realizing that I could have given birth to a child with medical problems made me much more willing to accept what

I did not know about our adoptive daughter. Any one of our other kids could suddenly come down with a serious illness or be diagnosed with a medical condition that I would not have knowingly accepted if I had the choice.

It was also helpful to understand that health is more of a continuum than a standard. Discussing our plan to adopt with our pediatrician, I had asked how best to avoid a child with fetal alcohol syndrome (FAS) or effects (FAE). He advised me not to be overly concerned about accepting a child who was at risk for either one. The range of symptoms, he said, was so huge that it would be practically impossible to know how much a child would be affected by such a condition. Many children had so few problems that there was no compelling reason to ever seek a diagnosis.

Love means committing to each other for better or for worse. Usually we get a portion of both. Both biological and adoptive families take risks with and for each other. There are no guarantees for the children we bring home from a hospital nursery or for those we bring home from a courtroom. Whether or not we fully know a child's past, we cannot know what the future holds or how that individual child will welcome it.

If medical mysteries stir up worry in your heart, just wait for the "angel" God sends in the people we love and trust. God will always give us the assurance we need to live out his divine will for us. The Holy Spirit will lead you through fear into faith. In doing so, God will establish in your heart love that cannot fail.

Think it through

❧ What level of uncertainty are you able to handle well?

❧ How do you usually find peace and security in an unpredictable situation?

❧ Are you afraid of any particular medical problems your adoptive child may have?

❧ Are you prepared to support your friend or family member in addressing any health issues that may arise unexpectedly?

Pray it through

HOLY SPIRIT, DIVINE HEALER, give health to us and to our children. As we follow your plan, help us to understand all the medical information we receive. Teach us to give more weight to a person than to a diagnosis. Give us the grace to know our limitations and the prudence to live within them. Guard us from fear and free us from anxiety. Encourage us in love. Strengthen our resolve to choose love, especially in the face of what is unknown to us. Enable us to trust you when there are risks. Lead us from fear into faith. Send us all the reassurance we need. Keep us, and the children you are keeping for us, in the shelter of your embrace. Amen.

CHAPTER 23

The Burden of History

Love Bears All Things

The woman conceived and bore a son; and when she saw that he was a fine baby, she hid him three months. When she could hide him no longer she got a papyrus basket for him, and plastered it with bitumen and pitch; she put the child in it and placed it among the reeds on the bank of the river.

— Exodus 2:2–3

Mordecai had brought up Hadassah, that is, Esther, his cousin, for she had neither father nor mother; the girl was fair and beautiful, and when her father and mother died, Mordecai adopted her as his own daughter.

— Esther 2:7

REFLECTION

Our God knows every burden we bear and all the sacrifices that have been made by us and for us. The Holy One knew the pain Jochebed felt when she placed her infant son afloat in a basket on the Nile. The Lord saw Mordecai's willingness to raise his young orphaned cousin Hadassah as his own daughter. The Almighty looks at each of us with compassion and stoops to care for us when no one else will. God sees our dilemmas and reaches toward us with love that leads.

Divine love leads us all. Love led Pharaoh's daughter to take an abandoned Hebrew boy as her son. Love led the King of Persia to choose Hadassah—that is, Esther—as his wife. And even more, love led Moses, a Prince of Egypt, to deliver his people from slavery, and Esther to defend her people as their queen. Both Moses and Esther were adopted children. Their origins were simply that, the place their lives began.

PERSONAL

When we first met Yulia, she walked into the room with attitude. She was an obvious limelighter, adept at getting the attention every orphanage child needed, but few ever got. Her techniques were both subtle and endearing. They were certainly effective on us! When we heard about Yulia's background, we knew why she had become so good at working a crowd. It was her way of exercising some control over her life. The orphanage director and our adoption facilitator summarized what they called Yulia's "social history." Neither of us was really sure what a "social history" was or how a two-year-old could have one. As they began to talk, however, we found out.

I suppose that in some ways Yulia's story inspired me. She was exactly the kind of child we had hoped to find, one who desperately needed what we had to give. While it was hard to choke back the tears, I could sense great hope for Yulia's situation. Realizing that we held the power to change her life was as humbling as it was exciting. All we had to do was act on the compassion that Yulia's story had enkindled in us.

The injustice this poor child suffered made us indignant at some level. But the little girl we saw dancing and twirling before us was not angry, although she had every right to be. She was as charming as any child—even as engaging as the ones we had left at home. Hearing Yulia's history was very sad indeed. At not even three years old, she had experienced far more than her share of grief. No child deserves that kind of life.

There was a tangible reticence among the orphanage staff in telling us about Yulia's past. It was almost as if they expected us to cross her name off our list. The picture the staff painted was not a pretty one, and they knew it. Yet the child standing in front of us, the little girl holding a hand as she walked around the room, was very pretty indeed. Despite the negative things we heard, in that moment it was clear to us that Yulia's past did not have to dictate her future. Where she came from did not have the power to determine where she was going because she was going with us.

PRACTICAL

It is important for prospective parents to remember that the reasons they are able to adopt a child are often very sad. Our children come to us from death, poverty, addiction, racism, sexism, abuse, neglect, irresponsibility, social policies, and even war. While most of us have not lived with any of those horrors, many of our adoptive children have. Adoption is the sweet fruit that miraculously falls from bitter trees.

None of us ends where we begin. Each of us carries the burden of a personal history, a burden that can and does influence how we see ourselves as well as the choices we make. But what we carry does not have to set our direction or course for the rest of our lives. The issues adoptive children face as they grow up depend on what is woven into their own personal stories. As families, our task is to help our children face those issues in healthy ways. Most of us will discover that the help of therapists, doctors, and clergy is necessary—and invaluable.

As our children come to terms with the fabric of their lives, some threads of color may be painful to hear or remember. Others will remain hidden from them and from us. The truth, however, can be received if it is told in love and heard together. The gift of family makes it possible for the beauty of the fabric as a whole to be seen and embraced.

Think it through

- Do you find it challenging to acknowledge or accept the realities of what your child has been through?

- Are you open to the assistance that a therapist, doctor, education specialist, teacher, or clergy member is able to offer your family? How will you determine when you or your child needs help?

- Think of something from your own past that you needed—or still need—to work through. Were there things that made that process easier or more difficult for you?

❧ What can you do to encourage your friend or family member to explore the resources they may need to address their child's emotional needs?

Pray it through

HOLY SPIRIT, FATHER OF THE POOR, inspire in us compassion for the weak. Show us your power to bring good from evil, joy from sorrow, healing and wholeness from pain. Keep us mindful of all who are in need, especially those to whom you have called us. Give us grace not to judge others by their personal histories. Help us not to be ashamed of them or for them. Teach us that the past does not have to dictate the future. Empower us to change that little piece of the world in which we live. Enable us, too, to be changed by those we meet. In sharing the truth, give us a glimpse of your hand at work in our children's lives. Weave us together as one family sharing an eternity that is yet to come. Amen.

CHAPTER 24

Birth and Adoptive Mothers

Love Reconciles

Jesus replied, "Who is my mother and who are my brothers?" And pointing to his disciples, he said, "Here are my mother and my brothers! For whoever does the will of my father in heaven is my brother and sister and mother."

— MATTHEW 12:48–50

Then the king said, "The one says, 'This is my son that is alive, and your son is dead;' while the other says, 'Not so! Your son is dead, and my son is the living one.'" So the king said, "Bring me a sword," and they brought a sword before the king. The king said, "Divide the living boy in two; then give half to the one, and half to the other."

— 1 KINGS 3:23–25

Reflection

Jesus asked the same question many adoptive families find themselves wondering. "Who is my mother, and who are my brothers and sisters?" The answer he gave was not as obvious as one might expect. The mother of Jesus is the one who hears the word of God and does it. (Probably the best description of Mary ever!) Those who do the will of the Father are brothers and sisters to the Son of God.

What Jesus was telling us is something that in all likelihood we already knew. Our eternal family is made up of the people who love and care for one another. Blood may be thicker than water, but love trumps them both.

In a strange way, the story of King Solomon's judgment tells us the same thing. In a dispute between two women over a baby, the true mother will give her child to another woman rather than see him divided. Real love is selfless.

Personal

As a mother, I could not imagine allowing a child to be neglected as our soon-to-be-adoptive daughter had been. The whole thing made me angry. While righteous indignation may have a place, mine was not so righteous. It was a struggle to keep myself from feeling intrinsically superior to Yulia's birth mother. I found it downright impossible to resist the temptation to blame her. The problem was that I had just enough information to know how Yulia had been treated, but not nearly enough information to understand why.

Still, there were pieces of Yulia's story that didn't make much sense to me at the time. Abortion is very common throughout Russia, and has been for many years. If a woman didn't want a child, there was a socially acceptable—if not morally acceptable—way out. By God's grace, Yulia's birth mother chose to give her life.

The real puzzle, though, was the dissonance in my own heart. I could have loads of compassion for a child, but simultaneously hold contempt for the woman who gave birth to her. I realized that in order to overcome my profoundly negative feelings toward Yulia's birth mother, I would have to move way beyond the facts. Instead of envisioning what I knew about her background, I began to use my imagination to fill in the gaps and create scenarios about what I didn't know. By thinking of her and praying for her by name, Yulia's birth mother became more human to me. Trying to get inside her mind, I've been able to give her a place in my heart.

The truth is that while I have mixed feelings about her, so does our daughter. Only after ten years did she even want to know her birth mother's name. Today she carries it in a heart-shaped locket. The process of healing is underway.

PRACTICAL

While it can be difficult for an adoptive family to accept, a child's birth parents are always part of his or her life. That is true whether or not they share an ongoing relationship, and whether or not the relationship has been positive or negative for the child. Doing what we can to keep a charitable view of an adopted child's family of origin affirms the child's whole identity.

The story of the two mothers in the court of Solomon can teach us something about the adoptive child's struggle with birth and adoptive parents. Unsure of who her mother really is, she imagines a dispute between the two women who claim her. Believing that only one woman can be her mother, the solution she constructs to the dilemma she faces demands that she is torn in two. The result can leave the child with a fragmented identity and divided loyalties.

The adoptive family must take up the challenge to think more creatively and flexibly. Many who have taken the path of open adoption do so beautifully. Parents who adopt don't need to compete with a child's birth parents for their love. There is room for us all. What they can do, however, is to think and speak kindly of their children's birth parents, and teach them to do the same. The result will be a whole child with two mothers, rather than two childless women.

Children need a mother to give them life, and a mother to give them love. These gifts are not necessarily given to a child by the same woman. Adoption is based on recognizing that possibility. Still, both women have a critical role to play. Both are the child's "real" mother. Children need a father to give them life, and a father to provide for them and protect them. These gifts, too, are not necessarily given to a child by the same man.

If the feelings you have toward your child's birth family are confused or conflicted, you have gained a window into the emotional life of your child. We need not feel threatened by the fact that our children were not born to us. Life and love are meant to go together. All who love give life. Those who give life, in some measure, also love.

Think it through

- What feelings do you have about your prospective child's birth mother and father?

- How much information about your child's birth parents will you share with your child, family members, and friends?

❧ If you were to write a letter to your child's birth parents, what would you say?

❧ How will you handle your natural curiosity about the birth family your friend or family member's adoptive child comes from?

Pray it through

HOLY SPIRIT, SPIRIT OF MEEKNESS AND HUMILITY, give us hearts that know and accept the truth about ourselves and eyes that see others the way you see them. Teach us how to forgive those who have hurt the children you have called us to love. Help us to be grateful for those who gave them life and bless them. Fill us with a willingness to understand the pain they may have suffered, too. Keep us from competing with them or considering ourselves superior to them in any way. Teach our children kindness and forgiveness through us. Transform all our lives by the power of your love. Amen.

CHAPTER 25

Identity and Name

Love Recognizes

The daughter of Pharaoh came down to bathe at the river, while her attendants walked beside the river. She saw the basket among the reeds and sent her maid to bring it. When she opened it, she saw the child. He was crying, and she took pity on him. "This must be one of the Hebrews' children," she said. . . . When the child grew up, [the woman] brought him to Pharaoh's daughter, and she took him as her son. She named him Moses, "because," she said, "I drew him out of the water."

— EXODUS 2:5–6, 10

The nations shall see your vindication,
and all the kings your glory;
and you shall be called by a new name
that the mouth of the LORD will give.

— ISAIAH 62:2

REFLECTION

Among the great heroes of the Bible, few names resound as powerfully as Moses. Yet, if we stop to think about it, we realize that Moses was the name given to Israel's deliverer by the daughter of Pharaoh. It was an Egyptian rather than a Hebrew name, given by the child's adoptive mother and not his birth mother. We will never know what Jochebed called him as she wrapped him in a blanket and set him afloat on the river. No name other than Moses is ever mentioned.

Throughout the Bible, God gives new names to people when the divine Initiator is doing something new. Abram and Sarai became Abraham and Sarah. Jacob became Israel. Simon was called Peter, and Saul became Paul. As Christians, we keep this tradition when we are given new names at Confirmation or at religious profession. These names express the new mission our Father envisions for us and are meant to inspire us to attain the holiness of those who answered to them before.

The prophet Isaiah tells us that God promises to give each of us a new name. While they are mysteries to us here, they are kept in the mouth of our heavenly Father. What we do know, however, is this: the names God gives us will reflect not only who we are, but also who we were made to become. We will be called by a name that announces we belong to the God of heaven. That glory will be the vindication of us all. And more, it will be our joy!

PERSONAL

As soon as our homestudy was underway, there was great interest and discussion in our house about what name we were going to give to the newest kid on the block. Everyone got into the act, and everyone had an opinion. One thing was non-negotiable for us: the name had to be Russian.

It didn't take long for Anastasia to rise to the top of our list. It sounded good, produced several possible nicknames, and belonged to one of the last Russian princesses. Best of all, Anastasia means "resurrection."

When we actually traveled to Russia, however, the rules of our name game changed rather abruptly. Deciding to adopt a toddler rather than an infant meant that our daughter already had a name—one that she used for herself and answered to. We couldn't imagine asking Yulia to answer to anything else. Her name was already too much a part of her emerging identity.

We decided that our best approach would be to extend Yulia to Juliana, and give her Christine as a middle name. In that way, Yulia could have a new name—one that we had given her—without losing the name she already had. Because "Anna" means "grace," we figured that what we were doing was adding the grace of Christ to Yulia. We continued to call her Yulia, but those extra syllables were there for her when and if she ever wanted them.

PRACTICAL

Names are important. If they weren't, we wouldn't have entire bookstore shelves filled with volumes offering advice and lists for naming your baby. And though I have never looked, I'm convinced that there must also be books out there written to help name your dog, cat, or goldfish too. ("Do you think 'Fluffy' is just too old-fashioned?") Parents—both birth and adoptive—give the matter of naming a child a great deal of attention. We do so because we know that names express identity. They reveal something about who we are, and whose we are as well. Even more, our names influence how we see ourselves.

Naming presents a unique set of considerations for families who adopt. Unless they are adopting a newborn, parents come to realize that giving an adopted child a name usually means changing one he or she already has. Prospective parents may choose a name for their child even before receiving a referral. For them, accepting a child for adoption means that they have found Jacob or Sophia. Many, however, wait until they meet their new son or daughter, and then try to find a balance between their own desires and what a child already brings with him or her.

Names, both old and new, express not only family ties, but also cultural connections. While maintaining a child's culture is a worthy pursuit, many adoptive families are careful to avoid any difficulties their children may have with their peers. Parents may decide to change a particularly unusual name, for example, to something less obtrusive. For me, Ivan would have been fine, but Igor? I don't think so.

Choosing to keep your child's name or trade it in for a new one is ultimately a matter of personal preference. The truth is that both old and new names can hold rich significance for a child. Parents may be less willing to name change if they know that it is their child's only possession, the only thing he really owns. Old names, too, can provide a sense of continuity for a child and security in his own identity. A new name, on the other hand, can help a child reinforce his belonging to a new family. For children coming from difficult backgrounds, a new name may reassure them that they are being given a whole new life.

Think it through

- What does *your* name mean? Does your name honor a particular culture, tradition, or person?

- Are you open to keeping the name your child already has?

- Have you already chosen a name for your child, or will you wait until you meet each other in person?

- Are you prepared to honor whatever choice your friends or family members make in naming their adoptive son or daughter?

Pray it through

HOLY SPIRIT, BREATH OF GOD, you call us each by name. Give us the grace to know who we are and to be fully who you created us to be. Help us to recognize your voice. Seal us as your own. Inspire us to give our children names they can embrace with all their hearts. Enable them to begin anew with the knowledge that they belong not only to us, but to you. Strengthen in them their identity as children beloved by the Father. Give them the certainty of our acceptance. Protect them from isolation. Build in them a strong sense of self. Help them to be proud not only of what they are called, but of whom they are called to be. Amen.

CHAPTER 26

The Waiting Child

Love Hopes

But you do see! Indeed, you note trouble and grief,
that you may take it into your hands;
the helpless commit themselves to you;
you have been the helper of the orphan.

— PSALM 10:14

Leave your orphans behind, I will keep them alive . . .
— JEREMIAH 49:11

REFLECTION

The Holy Spirit brings families and children together. He cares for both long before they meet. Our heavenly Father is the helper of orphans. He sees and attends to every trouble and grief. Anyone who is helpless can find help in him. God takes it all in his hands.

In fact, we can trust that even when we must leave them behind, they will be kept alive by the Spirit of God. Looking forward with faith to the day of our children's homecoming, we can begin to understand that we are merely sharing in what God has been doing all along in our absence. All our lives, God loves, cares, calls, and waits for each of us to come home to him.

Personal

Three days after we met Yulia, we returned to the orphanage to confirm our desire to adopt her. After we signed the orphanage book pledging ourselves to Yulia, the orphanage director took us upstairs to tell her that we would be her mama and papa. She told Yulia that she would have to listen to us, do what she was told, be a good girl, and keep herself clean. The director also explained that Yulia would have a family now and that we would soon come back to take her home. We gave Yulia the musical toy we had brought with us, as well as the "Who Loves Baby?" photo album with pictures of our whole family inside. As Yulia threw her arms around us, the orphanage director left the room. I sensed that even though there were 120 children living there, Yulia would be missed.

We returned to Russia less than a month later. Knowing that three weeks is an eternity to a child, we weren't sure how Yulia would respond to us. But, catching a glimpse of Andrew and me through a window, she burst through the door laughing so hard she could barely breathe. She was so excited she couldn't contain herself.

The director also told us that, during those intervening weeks, Yulia had stopped eating and would not let go of the toy and photo album we had given her. But the most amazing thing was how much Yulia's language had improved. The director told us that she had seen this happen before. Children who knew that they were going home often had a burst of development, especially in language. Talking had become more important to Yulia because now she had someone she wanted to talk to.

We returned to the orphanage to see Yulia as soon as we had completed our court proceedings on the following day. Yulia was more than ready to go home; she expected that we would be able to take her with us immediately. Unfortunately, that was not the case. There were several bureaucratic stops that we would have to make the next morning. In a flurry of activity, we needed to obtain our daughter's Russian passport, adoption certificate, and a new birth certificate that named us as her parents. When we told her that we would have to come back for her the next day, Yulia exploded into uncontrollable tears.

Holding her close, I repeated the Russian word for "tomorrow." After a few minutes she joined the mantra and calmed down. Reminding her she still had her photo book of family pictures seemed to help, too. As we left, I was the one who broke down. Obviously, the wait had been much harder on her than it could ever have been on us.

PRACTICAL

Few of us will ever fully appreciate what it is like living day to day in an orphanage, or in foster care, or to be without stable family relationships. Many children awaiting adoption are not exactly sure what it is they are waiting for. Still, I think children understand that there is no substitute for a family that loves them. Even if family life is completely foreign to them, even if past experiences of family relationships hurt them, kids know what they need.

Many adults have struggled through years hoping to have a baby. Adoptive parents pass months in anticipation of bringing a child home. But however long it takes for us our children have waited their entire lives to experience what it means to have a home. Every moment of their days has been spent wishing, perhaps unconsciously, for parents who are able to love them the way they need to be loved.

Think it through

- Do you believe your child is at risk of any harm while your adoption is still in process? Is there anything you can do to address that concern?

- Is there something you can leave with the child you are planning to adopt that can prepare him or her to be part of your family?

- Has waiting to be adopted been a conscious or even traumatic experience for your child?

- Is there something you can do to reduce the anxiety your family member or friend may feel during the final stages of the adoption process?

Pray it through

Holy Spirit, Spiritual Balm, you loved our children before we knew anything about them. Before we could care for them, you kept them alive. When others could not meet all their needs, you sustained them. Help us to think well of those who did their best to provide for our children before they were ours. Bless them in the demands of their daily work. Give them hearts of compassion for the children in their care. Help us to give our children the home they long for, the one they have waited for all their lives. When our love comes up short, fill in the gaps with the ointment of your mercy. Provide for us all from the richness of your grace. Amen.

Home Together

CHAPTER 27

A Brand New Shiny Life

Love Makes Everything New

"Arise my love, my fair one,
and come away;
for now the winter is past,
the rain is over and gone.
The flowers appear on the earth;
the time of singing has come . . ."

— SONG OF SOLOMON 2:10–12A

And the one who was seated on the throne said, "See, I am making all things new." Also he said, "Write this, for these words are trustworthy and true."

— REVELATION 21:5

REFLECTION

New love is a springtime in its own right. A new child in the family is reason to celebrate with joy. The "issues" we observe in those early days can wait. It won't be long until the challenges present themselves; adoptive parents do not need to search them out. We only need to observe and respond.

God celebrates each of us. The warm breath of the divine Spirit melts the winter of our icy souls. Our Father's presence is the seal of hope and the promise of new life. Coming away with the Lord, the rains end, the sun rises, and flowers appear. The deserts we have known burst into bloom. Our Father knows that the pain we experience in spiritual growth will come soon enough. The moment God first grasps us as his own is precious to him. It is a time for singing. And if we listen, we may even hear the sound of God's voice in the song.

PERSONAL

Arriving at the orphanage one day after our court appearance, we were ushered very quickly into a small hallway. Yulia was told to undress. The dress she had worn, the underwear, socks, and her little turquoise shoes were reluctantly given back to the orphanage. There was nothing for her to take with her except the musical toy and the photo album we had given her. Everything she owned had come from us.

There was little time for good-byes, as we were headed directly to the airport to catch the next flight to Moscow. Putting on her new coat and hat, Yulia waved as if she was going out to play. She did not seem to understand that she would never return.

Suddenly, Yulia was exposed to the world outside the orphanage. That world was very much bigger than she was prepared for.

Everything we did was new and strange. Cars, planes, foods, beds, toilets—nothing was the same. There was far too much to take in all at once. As a result, Yulia was on constant overload. She needed a great deal of reassurance. We had learned just enough Russian to get by and Yulia was eager to learn English. But the language barrier between us meant that physical affection and touch was the first and best mode of communication we had.

Those first few days together in Moscow were filled with discovery for Yulia and for us. Our daughter was delighted to go shopping, and all the clerks loved her. A street vendor was so enchanted by her that he gave her a small *matryoshka* or stacking wooden doll. Yulia danced with abandon in the streets of Moscow, singing a little nursery rhyme as she went and holding tightly onto my hand.

Food, too, was an adventure. At McDonald's she winced at the ice in her drink, tore the breading off her chicken nuggets, and had no use for fries. (My, how things change!) On the other hand, she couldn't get enough yogurt or eat too many apples. On one occasion, we ordered soup from room service, figuring that it would be familiar to her. Yulia promptly fished everything out of the soup, and ate only the broth. When we thought about it we realized that she had probably never seen anything *in* her soup.

Though she was friendly and generally well mannered, at times Yulia was hard to settle down. Within a few days she began testing our limits and stood up to me when I told her that she couldn't eat candy for supper. Repeating my instruction, she tried to get her way by manipulating me with smiles, giggles, and hugs. She was extremely frustrated to find that her technique didn't work.

During our time in Moscow, she tested our commitment to the rules on almost every issue involving parental authority. As tempting as it was to feel sorry for her and cave in, we stood firm. In all honesty, I was afraid not to. By the end of each day, I felt completely depleted. Fortunately, because life outside the orphanage was emotionally exhausting for Yulia, getting her to bed generally wasn't too difficult!

PRACTICAL

Newly adopted babies and children are a cross between bulls in a china shop and kids on Christmas morning. Everything stimulates them, everything excites them, and everything exhausts them. New parents can't help but follow the same pattern. Because lots of changes are being made in quick succession, there is a tendency to try to do everything at once. The work of learning to love and live with one another, however, takes time.

In the early days of being a family, it may be best to keep stress as minimal as possible. While everyone wants to meet your new son or daughter, they do not all need to rush into your child's life at once. It is important for us to remember that in coming home our children have also had to leave some things behind. While we may be on cloud nine, the recently adopted child may feel as if he or she is falling out of the sky. We just need to open our hearts wide enough to catch him or her.

Think it through

* What expectations do you have of your child's behavior during the first few weeks after your adoption?

* What new things do you think your child will find the most exciting?

* What unfamiliar things about your child's new life do you think will be the hardest for him or her to adjust to?

⫸ Is there anything you can do to help your friend or family member keep things as calm as possible during the first few weeks and months with their newly adopted child?

Pray it through

HOLY SPIRIT, EVERLASTING SPRING, you make everything new. In you all things come to color and life. Teach us to be fully present to the moment. Inspire us to discover one another, to unwrap the gift of being family. Help us to leave progress for another day. Give us joy in the miracle we have received, in promises made and fulfilled, in the journey's end that turns to new beginnings. Melt the winters our children have endured. Bring our hearts to singing and our souls to laughter. Keep the memory of these early days alive in us that we may draw strength from them as we learn to live and love together. Amen.

CHAPTER 28

Settling In

Love Guides

You have seen what I did to the Egyptians, and how I bore you on eagles' wings and brought you to myself. Now therefore, if you obey my voice and keep my covenant, you shall be my treasured possession out of all the peoples.

— Exodus 19:4–5a

REFLECTION

God rescued the children of Israel from slavery in Egypt. Empowering Moses to lead them, the Almighty brought his people to himself. Borne up on eagles' wings, they breathed the air of freedom for the first time in generations. Their Father gave them everything in advance. Only then did the Holy One ask them to obey his

voice and keep the covenant. If they chose to accept divine authority, they would be God's most treasured possession.

Our heavenly Father gives everything to us before he asks anything of us. God's commandments are always given in the context of
an ongoing and personal relationship. The Lord frees us for freedom. Reminding us of all that has been done on our behalf, God's
Holy Spirit waits for us to ask what we might do in return.

PERSONAL

The most dramatic change our new daughter had to make
involved the concept of freedom. Yulia had never actually been
allowed to decide anything. Her orphanage life had been regi-
mented in every way. The expectations of the orphanage caregivers
were clear. There was little spontaneity in play or in relationships.
Everything was organized and supervised. Nothing was left to
chance. She was told when to go, where to go, and what to do when
she got there. Mostly, she was led by the hand. Eventually, she was
even told to go with strangers she hardly knew to the opposite side
of the globe.

Very early on, we observed that Yulia did not know what to do
with the freedom our other children exercised without thinking. It
perplexed her so much that when offered a choice, she would
become so dazed that she could not make one. But it didn't take
long for Yulia to figure out that when she asked for something she
would get it. Suddenly there was no end to her asking. All she
wanted to do was have whatever she desired, simply because, for the
first time in her life, she could. Yulia would frequently have several
plates of different foods lined up in front of her chair. She didn't eat
many of them. She just wanted to exercise her options. After a while,
we exercised ours.

The concept of personal property was completely foreign to our daughter as well. This placed a particular strain on her relationships with her brothers and sisters. Because nothing had been hers before, Yulia was quick to say that *everything* she saw belonged to her alone. Our other children were not at all happy to hear the Russian word for "mine" sweepingly applied to things that belonged to them. Yulia did not know how to distinguish between what was communal property and what belonged to individuals in the house. Try as we did, there was no simple way to explain it. After a few rather difficult incidents, she knew better and did better.

While we had expected to encounter substantial adjustment issues, there were things missing from Yulia's orphanage life that had never crossed our minds. She had never been in a kitchen, never ridden in a car, never seen anything bought or sold. Because her diet was so poor, Yulia did not know what most fruits and vegetables were. She had never tasted most of them. To keep the children safe, the orphanage silverware was limited to spoons. Yulia had never even seen a fork, and for months after coming home she couldn't remember what to call it. She had heard a lot of crying babies all her life and had never been alone. She had felt hungry night after night when she went to bed, but didn't really know how to ask for food. On the other hand, she knew just what to do to steer a little attention in her direction when she wanted it—cuddles, kisses, and smiles may have been how she got more attention than other children at the orphanage. She also knew how to fly at altitudes well below adult radar. In short, Yulia knew a lot about how to survive, but not very much about how to simply live. It was obviously going to take time for her to get used to daily life in a family setting.

Practical

It does not take long for adoptive parents to figure out that they need to adjust almost as much as their new child. In truth, every family member will adapt not only to the newest addition, but also to the new dynamic that arises. This process is often slower than we would like it to be. It calls for more patience and more work than we might expect.

The most challenging thing for new families to establish is discipline. While most children we adopt have lived in an environment with rules and routines, few have any appreciation for parental authority. The adopted child's experience is largely limited to rules without relationship. Rules are made and enforced by whoever is "in power." Genuine authority, however, is personal. It can exist only in the context of an ongoing relationship.

An adoptive family may be the first stable set of interpersonal relationships some children have ever had. The stronger those relationships become, the more secure a child will feel. A child who trusts is able to accept authority and receive love.

Think it through

- What do you think are some differences between "power" and "authority"?

- What are the rules you expect your child to obey?

- How will you teach your child to respect others? What does "respect" look like to you?

- Is there something you can do to help your family member or friend establish some structure and routine with their new son or daughter?

Pray it through

HOLY SPIRIT, SPIRIT OF FREEDOM, write your law in our hearts. Show us how to be truly free. Help us to love what is good and right. Empower us to make choices according to your will. Teach us how to use authority well, to establish rules for the sake of relationships and to inspire mutual respect in our home. Guide our children toward security and trust. Help them to know that we will be faithful to them, that we will keep our word. Show us the adjustments we must make. Enable us to give ourselves fully to our children without the expectation of receiving their love in return. Amen.

CHAPTER 29

Being There

Love Is Always There

"I will not leave you orphaned . . ."

— John 14:18

"I will be with you; I will not fail you or forsake you."

— Joshua 1:5b

REFLECTION

God created us to be with him and with others. Our whole lives are really one extended opportunity for presence with one another and with him. That is why our Father continually gives us the assurance of his presence. The Holy Spirit does not fail us because he does not forsake us. The divine Spirit of adoption is the One sent to fulfill the promise Jesus made to his disciples when he said, "I will not leave you orphaned" (Jn 14:18).

All that we possess comes from God. But beyond what he has given us remains God himself. The divine Giver wishes, more than anything else, to give us his own life. Never abandoning us, God's presence heals the hurts each of us has suffered. Holding us in a mystical embrace, our heavenly Father teaches us to trust in his abiding love.

Personal

Yulia stuck to me like suction cups soaked in superglue and set in concrete. She followed me everywhere, at times so closely that I knocked her down just by turning around. I was the object of her every waking moment. She was more cautious with Andrew. But in a pinch, even he would do. Because all the orphanage workers were women, men were just one of those things she had to get used to. (I'm not sure I've completely adjusted to them!)

Though she was all smiles, it was evident that Yulia had a real fear of abandonment. Any time I left the house, she demanded reassurance that I would return. She maintained an unwavering surveillance of the front door. Every time I got near it, she required a hug and a kiss—even when I was just walking down to the end of the driveway to get the mail. There was no such thing as giving Yulia the slip—she always knew who was home and who wasn't. When anyone did come home, Yulia was the very first to greet them at the door.

Separation anxiety influenced a great deal of Yulia's behavior. It was the "man behind the curtain" whenever her Wizard of Oz appeared. What Yulia did was not particularly immature, but the way she did things revealed what an insecure child she was. Yulia did not know how to relax. Her muscles were always tense. She rushed into and out of just about every activity frantically, even frenetically at times. Above all, Yulia worried perpetually. It seemed as though she was afraid that someday she would wake up and find that coming home had only been a dream.

Yulia was determined to hold on to her new life with every bit of strength she had. She was far too scared to let go. Fear permeated her family relationships in those early weeks. It showed its face in unyielding perfectionism. If she made a mistake, Yulia was devastated. She simply could not trust that we would love her in spite of it.

Much of how our daughter acted felt odd to me; a good deal of it seemed quite irrational. I started to figure it out only when I realized that Yulia was probably doing what all of us do—acting out of her own life experience. I couldn't understand how the past was shaping her actions because I had not been a part of it. I hadn't been there with her.

PRACTICAL

No matter how experienced you are in child raising, there are some discipline techniques that may not be effective or appropriate with your newly adopted child. As a mother of seven children already, I was not fully prepared to completely retool my skills for number eight. I was certainly not willing to let our daughter make a transition from "poor orphan" to "spoiled brat." But seeing her fear of rejection and abandonment, I knew that things like "time out" were not at all appropriate. The last thing Yulia needed was to be sent away alone.

Other common methods don't offer the adoptive parent much help either. Spanking, even in moderation, is not a real option. Any child with a history of abuse cannot be taught by what may have, at another time, threatened his or her life. Depending on a child's pre-adoption background, even raising your voice can be destructive to long-term parenting goals. (That, in particular, has been very challenging for me.) Simply stated, deprivation doesn't work. A child who has had so little of what she needs is unlikely to be swayed by whatever you might take away from her. What, after all, can anyone take away from a child who at one time did not have a family? The truth is that most standard approaches to discipline undermine the trust that your child needs to build.

The answer is for parents to become creative and a little unconventional. We have found that just being there goes a long, long way. The best thing to do with bad behavior is to use it to reinforce, rather than threaten, family relationships. Taking Yulia in my arms and looking her in the eye, I calmly, but firmly, correct her. My temper doesn't make it easy for me to discipline in that way. But when I have been able to muster it, I have been far more successful.

Presence is the key to breaking the code of a child's behavior. It is the only way to heal the absences of the past that are so deep they can still be felt. Presence, in fact, is what draws our children out of their painful or disrupted pasts. In presence, our children begin to trust. In trust, they reach out to the future.

We give our children so many things. All of what they need and much of what they desire come as the result of our love for them. But if all that we have given them were to be lost, they would still have what they need most. They would have us. Ultimately, what our children want more than anything else is simply our presence. They want us to watch them, to hear them, to touch them. There is no mystery in that. It is because, like the rest of us, they want to be seen, heard, and touched.

Think it through

- ❧ Do you find it difficult to be fully present to another person? How can you practice being present?

- ❧ How do you intend to discipline your child? What will you do if that approach doesn't work?

- ❧ What can you do to help your child learn how to relax?

- ❧ Is there a way you can be more present to your friend or family member after the adoption has been completed?

Pray it through

HOLY SPIRIT, DIVINE PRESENCE, you have never failed or abandoned us. Help us to experience your abiding love, to sense that you are always with us, always for us, always among us, even within us. Show us how to be truly and actively present to our children. Teach us to watch them, to listen to them, and to touch them. Keep us from trying to substitute other things for our presence in their lives. Give us the answers to questions we never even imagined. Inspire creative approaches to challenging behavior. Enable our children to accept our presence in their lives. Inspire in their young hearts, and ours, fresh hope for the future. Amen.

CHAPTER 30

Bonding and Attachment

Love Bonds

Yet it was I who taught Ephraim to walk,
I took them up in my arms;
but they did not know that I healed them.
I led them with cords of human kindness,
with bands of love.
I was to them like those
who lift infants to their cheeks.
I bent down to them and fed them.

— Hosea 11:3–4

I thought how I would set you among my children,
and give you a pleasant land,
the most beautiful heritage of all the nations.
And I thought you would call me, My Father,
and would not turn from following me.

— Jeremiah 3:19

Reflection

Whether we know it or not, God has loved us from the start. It was the Lord who taught us to walk. It was the Father who took us in his arms to heal us when we were hurt. We moved along paths led by divine kindness. Never directionless, the Eternal drew us on with bands of love. When we were hungry, God bent down to feed us. When we were low, our heavenly Father lifted us up to the radiance of his face.

Still, not all of us have responded to God's love with love in return. Refusing to call God our Father, many have turned from following his Sprit. Set among his children, some have simply chosen to remain alone. God has experienced the disappointment of unrequited love. Still, there is always hope in heaven. For as long as the Father continues to love us as children, we may yet bond our hearts to his.

God's whole purpose for our lives has to do with bonding. Our heavenly Father is completely attached to us. His greatest desire is for us to choose intimacy with him. All the love we have ever experienced comes from the Creator, so much so, in fact, that we can say that wherever love is, there is God.

Personal

Mary may have had a little lamb, but we had Yulia. She followed us everywhere, from room to room, upstairs and down, from chair to couch and back. No one could get rid of her, not even by going to the bathroom! We knew that bonding would take time, but we didn't expect that it would be so aggravating. While we appreciated Yulia's affection, we wished that it would come in smaller doses. There were times I just wanted to push her away. Sometimes I did.

There were other instances, however, when Yulia pulled away from me. She had an amazing capacity to look in every direction other than mine when she didn't like what I was telling her. If I demanded eye contact, she simply closed her eyes, and poof—I disappeared! Yulia needed and demanded a lot of physical affection. We began to notice, however, that she only accepted affection on her terms. When she asked to be held, she was happy. If I picked her up, she squirmed.

On the other hand, Yulia didn't seem to understand how intimate a relationship was or should be. She was often indiscriminate—and inappropriate—with her affection. I knew that something had to give when Yulia ran up to a Home Depot employee and hugged him around the legs. Clearly, boundaries needed to be set and respected.

Establishing boundaries was difficult because most of the adults she flirted with welcomed the attention she gave them. I tried to rein her in by explaining how unsafe it was for her to be so trusting of strangers. Most of the adults just responded by introducing themselves. What finally worked was coming up with a way for Yulia to physically connect with people she met, but at an acceptable level. When the instruction finally sank in, Yulia learned to give the most enthusiastic handshakes ever!

Practical

Bonding is a process that is undertaken by every family member. Babies begin to bond to their parents even before birth. Sounds, warmth, nurturing, and all kind of physical sensations work together to establish a lasting connection between children and their parents. Newborns respond to the voices of their mothers and fathers. Brothers and sisters cuddle and play, interacting with familiarity and delight. Grandparents *ooh* and *ah*, hold and caress and "spoil" their grandchildren with attention. We all learn the meaning of intimacy through experience. Little by little, day after day, people become attached to one another by bonds meant to last a lifetime.

The ability to bond makes it possible for us to both give and receive love. Difficulties arise when the natural process of bonding is disrupted or incomplete. That is why healthy attachment is not a given for the adoptive child. Bonding is strengthened whenever a child has a need, expresses that need, and has it filled by a loving adult. When needs are unexpressed or unmet, the cycle is broken.

Love is usually a response to love. Adoptive parents should expect to "front" a tremendous amount of love and affection for their new son or daughter without anticipating an immediate return. Eye contact, physical touch, sweets, and even bottle-feeding have been helpful tools for families seeking to aid the bonding process.

While an adoption decree grants custody and legal responsibility, it cannot create personal attachments. There is no getting around the fact that adoptive parents and their children start out as strangers. To the extent that they bond to one another, they become a family. Unless parents and children risk genuine attachment, they cannot give or receive genuine love. For many adoptive families bonding is a lifetime work-in-progress. Still, it is never too late to open one's heart to another.

Think it through

- Are there some simple things you can do to encourage or support the process of bonding with your child?

- Have you had difficulty establishing healthy boundaries in relationships or been afraid of intimacy?

❧ What are the characteristics you value most in your closest relationships?

❧ How long do you think it will take for your family members or friends to bond with their child?

Pray it through

HOLY SPIRIT, SPIRIT OF BELONGING, draw our hearts toward one another in love. Enable us to act tenderly, even when it is inconvenient. Help us to recognize our children's need for affection. Show us how to use everything in our lives to grow in intimacy. Keep us from pushing our children away. Guide us, and them, in drawing healthy boundaries and attachments. Make us a family bound by love, conscious of one another's needs and desires. Give our children the grace to receive love and then to be able to give love in return. Lead us all by your kindness, and raise every one of us to the Father's face. Amen.

CHAPTER 31

Traveling Heavy

Love Comforts

"I am the Lord, and I will free you from the burdens of the Egyptians and deliver you from slavery to them. I will redeem you with an outstretched arm and with mighty acts of judgment. I will take you as my people, and I will be your God."

— Exodus 6:6–7

But I have calmed and quieted my soul,
like a weaned child with its mother;
my soul is like the weaned child that is with me.

— Psalm 131:2

REFLECTION

God did not deliver the Israelites from bondage in order to abandon them in the desert. The God of Abraham, Isaac, and Jacob called their children out of Egypt to make them a chosen people all his own. Moses was the outstretched arm of God. Through his anointed agent of redemption, God brought Israel forth with mighty acts of power. The Lord freed them from slavery, from all the burdens they had borne in bondage. The Book of Exodus recounts how God's promise was also his plan.

Yet, as difficult as it was to take the Israelites out of Egypt, it was even harder to take Egypt out of the Israelites. For forty years they wandered, still nostalgic for the security they left behind and the onions that grew along the Nile. Only afterward were they prepared to inherit what had been promised to them from the beginning.

Contentment is the gift of a peaceful spirit. As parents, we know that one of the best things we can hope for our children is that they make enough peace with their lives to find peace in their hearts. The image of the weaned child sitting calmly on his mother's knee captures the essence of that hope. A child fully nurtured is a child fully at rest.

Our God is not only a Father who delivers us, but also a Mother who nurtures us. The Lord offers each of us a strong arm and a tender breast. The Holy Spirit frees us from the burdens we carry. Leading us out of bondage and distress, God feeds us with the milk of divine presence.

PERSONAL

Because we had no delusions about being fashionable, we traveled to Russia with as little luggage as possible. At least, that is what we thought. As it turned out, however, we discovered that Yulia had more baggage than we did. Neither of us could see what she was carrying, but we could tell that it was pretty heavy.

Yulia's moods were like tides. Suddenly and without warning, she could be subject to a wave of emotion so strong that it would carry her out to sea beyond our grasp. Sometimes we felt as if all we could do was stand on the beach, throw her a line, and hope to pull her back to shore. It was clear that beneath the surface, our daughter was dealing with a constant undercurrent of emotional distress.

Yulia's distress showed itself in many ways. While I had spoken to her exclusively in Russian for the first few weeks at home, she was terrified if anyone else spoke Russian to her. Yulia was also a first-class pack rat. She stashed cookies, raisins, meat sticks, candies, cheese, juice boxes—you name it—in dresser drawers, the closet, and innumerable bags and purses. And, though she was a daring and adventurous child, Yulia cried frequently, intensely, and at the drop of a hat.

I couldn't always figure out why Yulia acted the way she did. The fact that I had no clue about what to do or how to help her frustrated me. Realizing that there would be times I wouldn't be able to help her made me sad. But as I observed Yulia more and more, I understood that she was simply trying to unpack her bags. I also began to understand that our job was to prepare her to sort through what she had brought with her when—and only when—she was ready to do so.

PRACTICAL

Most adoptive children are anything but calm, at least in the beginning. Their souls are scattered, not collected. Their hearts are restless rather than quiet. While we may want to focus our energy on weaning them from the past, we ought to understand that many of our children have had far too little time "at the breast." A child can only be weaned after he or she has been adequately nurtured.

All of us carry our emotional baggage with us. Burdens we pick up over the course of our lives are not easily laid down. Sometimes we are afraid to let go of them, because if we do we won't have anything to hang on to at all.

Adoptive children come with a whole set of luggage, some of it their own, some of it passed on to them by others, and some that even we may give them. Children experience their emotional distress differently. Some feel the strain of carrying it quickly and all at once. Others become conscious of it only after years of dragging it around.

While none of us want to see our children's pain, it is important for adoptive parents to know that their child's emotional needs provide an opportunity for bonding. Your children's inner struggles cannot be magically fixed overnight. Some may never be fixed at all. With patience and sensitivity, however, you will not only help them face what hurts, you will be there to face it with them.

Think it through

❧ Is there someone you can confide in about the emotional needs you will encounter in your child?

❧ Do you have "baggage" that you have been unable to unpack or let go of?

❧ How will you tell the difference between what you can and should do to help your child and what you just can't "fix"?

❧ Are you willing and able to refrain from comparing your friend's or family member's adopted child to other children you know, especially when it comes to behavior?

Pray it through

HOLY SPIRIT, SPIRIT OF GRACE AND PRAYER, we come to you for strength and comfort. Help us to go gently with one another. Show us how to lighten the burdens our children carry. Teach us how to weather the storms in their souls. Guide us in riding the waves and calming the winds that blow hard against them. Give us the wisdom to know when to be firm and when to be flexible. Fill us with sensitivity and patience. Empower us to face our children's hurts with them. Free us all from the heavy loads we bear, transform them into vehicles of your grace alive in us. Nurture us to contentment and bring our hearts to rest. Amen.

CHAPTER 32

Healing Love

Love Welcomes

But to all who received him, who believed in his name, he gave power to become children of God, who were born, not of blood or of the will of the flesh or of the will of man, but of God.

— John 1:12–13

"Anyone who welcomes one such child in my name welcomes me."

— Matthew 18:5

REFLECTION

Power to be in relationship flows both from receiving and believing. In receiving the Son, we come into relationship with the divine Being. We receive God's receiving of us. The Lord gives us power to become his children. That power is more than birth, or blood, or the human will can attain. It is the force of the very will of God that makes it possible for us to believe.

The words of Jesus echo through the Gospel: when we accept a child as she is, one "such as this," we welcome Christ himself. There is no greater blessing adoption can bring to us. The truly wonderful thing, however, is greater still. When our children so willingly accept us as we are, they give us the healing love we need. In us, they encounter the very same Jesus we welcome in them.

PERSONAL

The truth is that we didn't know how to handle Yulia at times. It was difficult to find a way to accept her without validating behavior that was not at all acceptable. Yulia desperately wanted to fit in and be good; she just didn't know how. Struggling to come up with a winning strategy, it became apparent that Yulia wasn't really able to take much of anything in stride. She had been deeply wounded.

I was more than willing to accept Yulia's background. In retrospect, though, I realize that I was a lot less willing to accept the damage her past had caused her. What she had suffered was behind her. The fact that she continued to be affected by it—well, that was another matter. It took a while for us to understand that although we had expected scars, Yulia still had open wounds. None of the band-aids in our medicine cabinet were the right size. And even if they had been, we didn't have nearly enough of them. After several months had passed, we had resigned ourselves to muddling through whatever our daughter presented to us.

One particularly challenging day, however, everything changed. For most of the morning it had seemed that Yulia's emotional kettle was about to boil over. After correcting yet another misbehavior, I picked our daughter up and cradled her. Within minutes Yulia's floodgates opened; she sobbed for more than twenty minutes. Yulia cried so hard that I shuddered at what anyone might think if they heard her. Her cries were not like anything I had ever heard—even from her. They came from the core of her being, from the place she hurt most of all. When she finally stopped, Yulia calmed down. Exhausted, she fell asleep.

Every day for the next few weeks, Yulia asked to be held. Taking our daughter in my arms, I encouraged her to cry out her grief. At times, I cried right along with her. Reflecting on what little I knew about her short life, I realized that most of what had happened to Yulia gave her plenty to cry about.

After some time, Yulia cried less and talked more. Recounting incidents from her past, she described rooms and faces and events in vivid detail. Even though some of what she talked about seemed to predate her time in the orphanage, it was as fresh to her as the present moment. More than simply remembering her past, Yulia was reliving it. As memories flooded into her mind, tears ran down her cheeks. These tears were not ordinary in any way. They were old tears, healing tears. She had stored them up until she felt safe enough to release them. I count them as precious as any gift I have ever received.

PRACTICAL

Accepting a child means accepting all that has wounded him or her. Parents should be prepared to recognize that some of the behaviors they'd like to change flow from the hurts their children have suffered. Hardest to accept, I think, is knowing that we can do so little about them. While it is tempting to sweep a child's woundedness under the rug, or trust that time will heal all, it is far better to accept the full force of our children's past hurts. Enduring pain is not the same as accepting it. If presence leads to trust, acceptance gives hope for healing.

When we fully accept our children as they are, we free them to become more fully themselves. Once brought into the light, the injuries we sustain can become secret passageways to our deepest fulfillment. The little boy who knows loneliness becomes a loyal friend. The girl who understands rejection welcomes others without reservation. Children who have lived in fear become pillars of strength and consolation. Drawing on the wounds we bear, we become better than whole.

Not every hurt can be healed completely. But those that linger in the children we love stretch our hearts more broadly and more deeply. If children teach us anything, they teach us to love past the horizon and beyond the shallows. After all is said and done, adoption is a vehicle of healing love.

Think it through

- ❧ How is "healing" different from "fixing"?
- ❧ Is there any woundedness you see in your child that you find particularly challenging to accept?
- ❧ Have any of the injuries you have suffered contributed to your character in a positive way?
- ❧ What small gesture of loving support could you do for your friends or family members that would make them and their child feel welcome and accepted?

Pray it through

HOLY SPIRIT, SPIRIT OF WELCOME, you do not reject anyone who comes to you. Help us to receive one another as we are. Show us how to fully accept our children the way they have come to us. Teach us to love them unconditionally and without reserve. Open our hearts to their wounds. Help us to listen to their pain and share it. Guide our children through their grief. Give us all the gift of tears that heal. Transform our injuries into victories and our hurts into gifts. Sustain us in hope. Empower us to believe. Through the love you have inspired, heal us all. Amen.

CHAPTER 33

No News or Good News?

Love Speaks

"Which one of you having a hundred sheep and losing one of them, does not leave the ninety-nine in the wilderness and go after the one that is lost until he finds it? When he has found it, he lays it on his shoulders and rejoices. And when he comes home, he calls together his friends and neighbors, saying to them, 'Rejoice with me, for I have found my sheep that was lost.'"

— LUKE 15: 4–6

REFLECTION

Our Master has many sheep. Each and every one of them is uniquely precious and irreplaceable. When one is missing, our Lord leaves the rest of the flock behind to find it. The divine Shepherd scours the wilderness. Searching every cave and canyon, the Holy

One refuses to return empty-handed. When the Shepherd has found what is lost, he carries it in his arms. Arriving home, he announces the good news. God cannot contain himself, for what was lost has been found. Together, all the host of heaven rejoice.

From God's point of view, human history reads like a sequence of lost and founds. Our Lord is one that seeks out the lost. At one time or another each of us falls into the pit of that category. God always knows where we are, even if we haven't quite figured out just how far we've wandered away. There is nothing our Father will not do to find us, no length to which he will not go to bring us home in his arms. All that belongs to heaven ultimately returns there. Our Father turns every losing into finding. We are the cause of God's joy.

Joy is meant to be shared and it multiplies in the sharing. Not every crevice and bramble needs to be recounted in the telling of our tales, for the heart of salvation's story does not change. Each of our lives testifies to the truth that all that is lost can be found. All that is missing can and will be restored. There is no greater cause for celebration.

Personal

All of our friends and relatives, and most of the people we dealt with on a daily basis, knew that we were in the midst of adopting a child. Some people shared how they had toyed with the idea of adopting a child themselves. Others were intrigued with how we came to the decision to adopt. Many asked heartfelt questions.

There were, however, a completely other class of people who were downright nosey. While they were not a regular part of our lives, they had no trouble prying into our lives. One woman inquired as to what our adoption cost. Another asked explicitly about Yulia's background and her "real" mother. (That, by the way, would be me.)

Generally, we've used a few tactics of escape and evasion to avoid answering questions that people should have known better than to ask. We also trained our older kids how to recognize an inappropriate question and just not answer any that fell into the all-you-ever-wanted-to-know-about-my-adopted-sister-and-were-brazen-enough-to-ask category. One of the best ways to guard Yulia's privacy was to keep her brothers and sisters on a need-to-know basis. Our other children don't really need to know every detail of Yulia's past.

Adoption is part of our family's history, but mostly, it belongs to Yulia. She, after all, is the only one to have experienced life on both sides of that watershed event. Respecting our daughter's right to tell her own story is something we consider critically important. Now that she's old enough, she's been able to share some of it herself.

PRACTICAL

Parents have very different opinions about who and how much to tell about their child's adoption. Some make their family history a kind of public scrapbook. Others guard their child's adoption as a family matter. A child adopted in infancy will need time to understand the role of adoption in his own life. A child who is older at the time of her adoption may need to grieve what has been lost from a former life. And, while it is increasingly rare, some children do not know that their parents are adoptive rather than biological.

While we haven't hidden the fact that Yulia came to us through adoption, we have tried not to make it a primary topic of discussion either. Adoption just doesn't seem to follow naturally from a conversation about the weather. Our goal has been to treat adoption as normal, because it actually is.

That being said, not every family has a choice. "Obviously" adoptive families tend to attract busybodies. Racial and cultural differences seem to make some people think they have a right to ask the details of a person's life story. It is possible to fend them off without being too rude. Often, a good sense of humor is the best defense.

No matter where you stand on the matter, the same basic principle applies: not everything is everyone's business. Those who share information should tell their stories without any pressure. Those who withhold information should do so without feeling any shame. However you choose to handle information about your child's adoption, you ought to handle it with and not just for your child.

The adoptive family may find it helpful to reflect on the difference between private and personal. An adoption cannot be purely private as it is a matter of public record and civic courts. Adoption is however, an intensely personal affair. We often forget that personal means having to do with a person; a real human being who belongs, as we all do, to the family of humanity.

Think it through

- Is there a difference between private and personal for you? If so, what is it?

- Who "needs to know" in your circle of family and friends? How much do they need to know?

- What will you use to guide you in speaking about your child's adoption comfortably, but within appropriate boundaries?

⋙ Is there something you can do or say to encourage others to respect the dignity and privacy of the child your friends or family
members have adopted?

Pray it through

HOLY SPIRIT, SPIRIT BEARING WITNESS to our souls, help us to
tell the story of your love with our lives more than with our words.
Show us how to preserve our children's dignity. Teach us to direct
our joy. Keep us from volunteering too much information to those
who do not need to know. Guide us in setting appropriate boundaries and help us to respect them. In celebrating our children's
homecoming, give us discretion and modesty. Make us sensitive to
our children's need for privacy and to their desire for intimacy.
Amen.

A Lifetime for Love

CHAPTER 34

The "Blending" Family

Love Grows

"I have other sheep that do not belong to this fold. I must bring them also, and they will listen to my voice. So there is one flock, one shepherd."

— JOHN 10:16

Then Peter began to speak to them: "I truly understand that God shows no partiality."

— ACTS 10:34

REFLECTION

The flock of the Shepherd comes from many pastures. From all the grasslands, fields, and hills God calls each sheep by name. We may not recognize the sound of every bleat or the color and texture of every woolen coat. Still, all sheep know the voice of the Lord who calls them. Finally brought together—gathered in one place—they know that they belong to him.

While we may expend our effort trying to figure out who belongs and who doesn't, the Holy Spirit works to make us a single flock. The Spirit of God seeks to unite us under the one true Shepherd. Saint Peter discovered that God has no favorites and shows no partiality. That is because God gives each of us all of his love. None of us requires preferential treatment. We need not worry about being treated fairly, for each of us is uniquely favored. God sees us all as belonging to him, not one any more than another. That belonging is the deepest thing we share and the loveliest gift we can give to one another.

Personal

Although she shared our last name and lived at our address, it took a while for me to feel as if Yulia was mine. Even though we had a court decree stating that she belonged to us, to me it still felt as if Yulia was someone else's child.

Initially, it seemed that way to our other kids too. Yulia looked a lot like them. She had a personality that meshed well with the rest of theirs. But when Yulia first came home, she was more of a guest than a sister. She wasn't quite one of the gang.

Language wasn't the only thing foreign about how Yulia communicated. The real difference was in how our children interacted with each other. Yulia had no idea how to have a brother or be a sister. While there were certainly enough other children with her at the orphanage, relationships between the children there had always been mediated by an adult. Here, she had to find her place and learn how to hold onto it.

Our family had fit together just fine before Yulia arrived. When she came home, we realized that the puzzle of household personalities would have to make room for an entirely new and different piece. Trying to figure out just where she fit in wasn't always easy, especially when the other pieces were disrupted. Sometimes it seemed as if Yulia was part of a whole different picture.

The challenges of blending are unique to each family. Still, every family can and does form a unified and beautiful whole. While all five of Al and Mary's children were adopted, they came from very different cultural and racial backgrounds. That presented unique challenges whenever they were out together in public. When the two adults nearby don't look anything like you, and no one suspects that the other kid you're with is your brother and not just your friend, things can be a bit difficult to explain. It isn't always the adoptive child that has trouble fitting in either. After years of infertility, Emily and Ian's family first adopted a daughter from China. A few years later, the three of them welcomed a biological child. In their household, pregnancy and childbirth were novel and unfamiliar.

PRACTICAL

As parents of "blended families," most of us try very hard to treat our biological and adoptive children equally. While many may think that biological children are the natural beneficiaries of preferential treatment, often it is our adoptive children who end up with the biggest slice of the attention pie. In trying to be fair, parents should let go of the notion that they can be absolutely equal with their children. Kids have different needs. A piano costs more than a clarinet, and a shoe size twelve double E will take more time to find than a seven medium. An adopted child's needs may look and feel more immediate or more intense. That can distract us from the fact that every child has needs—those we birth as well as those we adopt.

It can also make us lose sight of the reality that we parents have legitimate needs, too!

When it comes to our emotions, it is helpful to know that affection for our adoptive children grows. Guilt has no place here. Adoptive parents shouldn't expect to feel as "in love" with a newly adopted son or daughter as they do with the children they already have. Any disparity you notice has little to do with birth. It's all about bonding and time. In time your attachment will grow stronger, and the sparkle in your eye will shine more brightly. On a day in the not so distant future, you will notice that the affection you have for all your children is pretty much the same. In the meantime, bonding is encouraged and strengthened when parenting flows from the decision to love rather than from how parents may feel about that decision on any given day.

Think it through

❧ What is your family's biggest challenge to "blending"?

❧ Is there something you can do to help you balance how your children's needs are expressed and met?

❧ What is the most beautiful aspect of your family life?

❧ How can you help your family members or friends address their own legitimate needs as well as their children's?

Pray it through

HOLY SPIRIT, SPIRIT OF ONENESS, you bring many together as one flock. Move to unite us in your love. Help us to both give and accept the gift of belonging. Enable us to make our lives truly inclusive. Bridge every difference, every disparity, every distance between our hearts. Teach us patience with one another. Show us how to bend toward one another, to be more who we are because of one another. Help us to be fair to all our children. Keep us from partiality of any kind. Empower us to give all our love to each child. Gather us together as one family, sharing a common identity and life in you. Amen.

CHAPTER 35

Tough Questions

Love Is Truthful

Nicodemus said to him, "How can anyone be born after having grown old? Can one enter a second time into the mother's womb and be born?" Jesus answered, "Very truly I tell you, no one can enter the kingdom of God without being born of water and Spirit. What is born of the flesh is flesh, and what is born of the Spirit is spirit. Do not be astonished that I said to you, 'You must be born from above.'"

— John 3:4–7

REFLECTION

There are mysteries of origin and intimacy that we all find difficult to understand. The question Nicodemus poses to Jesus is as sincere as it is rhetorical. His question is not at all foreign to adoptive children and their parents. "How can anyone be born again? Is it possible for one to enter into his mother's womb a second time?" These questions are very real for the sons and daughters we adopt. They wonder, as do we, how it is that they might yet be "born" of us.

Jesus takes Nicodemus seriously and treats him sensitively. That is because our God takes questions. Whatever troubles us, whatever it is we long to know, God will hear and answer us. We may not completely understand what we hear. We may only be able to receive one small piece at a time. Nevertheless, our Father is ever attentive. Listening to the deepest questions of our hearts, the Holy Spirit witnesses the enduring power of new birth in each one of us.

Personal

When anyone asked our two youngest daughters where they're from, one used to say "Russia," and the other said, "Mommy's tummy." (Not exactly the answers people expect!)

Children have rather fragmentary understandings of their own origins. Our adoptive daughter, however, has had a few more variables to fit into her equation than her other brothers and sisters. Trying to exercise her powers of logical thinking, Yulia came up with more than a few explanations about where she came from and how she got here. Because she never remembered having any family in Russia, Yulia concluded at one point that she had mystically popped out of the orphanage walls.

While Yulia used to be less than certain about her origins, her younger sister seemed to have it all figured out. Weaving a fantastic (and completely fictional) plot, she told me that Yulia's family in Russia had died. With great compassion, she talked about how Yulia had found her way on foot to the orphanage because she wanted a family. In her version, the baby house was a place where her sister's wish came true. All that the story was missing was the "once upon a time" at the beginning and the "happily ever after" at the end. I wish it had all been that sweet.

Yulia's confusion about past relationships was evident in funny ways. About a year after she came home, I received an e-mail from a woman who had adopted a little girl from the same Voronezh orphanage that our daughter had come from. As it turned out, it was actually one of the little girls we had met along with Yulia. Marina had come home about a month after we had arrived with Yulia. At the time, Yulia was very excited to see Marina's photo. After quite a round of jumping up and down, she promptly asked if Marina was her sister!

PRACTICAL

Adoptive children have just as many questions as biological children. To us as parents, however, it may seem as though they have more questions simply because we have fewer answers. When our sons and daughters ask about where they came from, it is important that we go back beyond the time we first met them. It is not uncommon for adoptive children to think of themselves as never having been born. If the story we tell them starts somewhere in chapter two, it's easy to understand why they come to that conclusion. Every child comes into the world in the same way. Our adoptive children need to know that they are no different from anyone else in that respect.

The child of adoption has the great task of integrating two identities, and possibly even two very different lives. Parents can help their children do that by affirming the whole story. You need not provide more detail than is necessary, nor fill in missing information with conjecture. But when your child asks, you must tell the truth.

Thankfully, it is possible to tell it in bite-sized, age-appropriate, and life-affirming pieces.

Children do not need the complicated terminology adults use to avoid making judgments. They should not, however, be made to feel that their own life histories are open to appraisal or criticism. While we might anticipate a series of follow-up questions, most children will take what they hear from us as an organic whole. Very few will analyze their stories bit by bit. A child takes his or her cue more from how we tell things than from what we have to say.

Adoptive parents should expect to answer the same set of questions again and again. Asking for the same information does not suggest that your son doesn't believe what you've told him; nor does returning to the same questions indicate that your daughter has rejected you in any way. As children grow in maturity, they will be able to absorb aspects of their personal histories differently. And even if our kids remember our every word, they need the reassurance that comes from hearing the tale repeated. Throughout your child's life, the same questions and answers will continue to hold something new for the journey toward identity and self-discovery.

Think it through

- ❧ Where do you begin your child's life story when you share it?

- ❧ Can you tell your child what you know about his or her life without making judgments or encouraging your child to do so?

- ❧ Are you comfortable answering your child's questions with "I don't know"?

- ❧ Has your friend or family member's child ever asked you about his or her life story? What are the answers you gave or would give?

Pray it through

HOLY SPIRIT, SPIRIT OF REVELATION, you show us the truth in ways we can receive it. Help us to answer the questions our children ask with both honesty and love. Guide us in revealing to them the stories of their lives in ways that affirm their lives as a whole. Show them that you have been present with them from the start, that you heard their needs and brought them home in love. Keep them from feeling guilt or responsibility for whatever happened to them. Protect them from anger. Lead them on the path of self-discovery. Help them to accept who they are and to become who you have created them to be. Amen.

CHAPTER 36

A Language of Love

Love Is Gentle

Yet the number of the people of Israel shall be like the sand of the sea, which can neither be measured nor numbered; and in the place where it was said to them, "You are not my people," it shall be said to them, "Children of the living God."

— Hosea 1:10

Reflection

The children of Israel became more numerous than the grains of sand on the shore; the people God chose had grown into a mighty nation. Yet, at a particular latitude and longitude in their history, they did not belong. At a place deserted and without hope—perhaps at a place in their hearts—they heard words that negated their very existence: "You are not my people."

The very same place of desolation could become a place of security and joy. God's word could make the difference. If the Almighty said to them, "Children of the Living God," that alone would make them so. With a second word, they could be God's people again.

Through experience, Israel discovered that who they actually were depended completely on who God said they were. The divine word was truth. It still is. The language of the Holy Spirit is a lexicon of love. In God's grammar, we are always the object—the recipients—of his loving action. Every sentence is in the active voice. Every verb is in the present tense. There is no third person, no one outside the dialogue of belonging, for all our hearts belong to the Father who calls us his children. If only we could learn to speak God's language of love to ourselves and to one another!

Personal

Watching Yulia acquire a new language was fascinating. Before we even left Moscow she had learned a few English words, and her Russian had begun to lose the luster of its native tones. While I hoped that she would become bilingual, that just simply didn't happen. Yulia's understanding of English improved daily, but her ability to speak in Russian declined right alongside it. There was one week in which Yulia understood both languages, but couldn't really speak in either. That, I believe, was when she made her linguistic crossover. Afterward, Yulia was an English-only child. For her, getting a new mother meant gaining a new mother tongue as well.

Adoption adds new members to our families and new words to our personal lexicons. Not everyone we encounter, however, will speak the same language. The words people use reveal their inner dispositions and attitudes. This is particularly clear when the subject of conversation is adoption. If I had a quarter for every time someone asked me how much I knew about Yulia's "real" mother, I would be a rich woman indeed. Usually, I let it go. But in my mind's eye I imagined telling them that they were looking at Yulia's real mother and that I hadn't felt particularly fake when I got up that morning! Even more bothersome was being asked—in front of our children—which kids were my "own." My impish self would have loved to inquire if they thought that I had kidnapped someone else's child or just picked one up while shopping. Bread, milk, someone else's child . . . these supermarkets really do have everything!

Other phrases are a lot subtler though, and more insidious. After we had brought Yulia home, I noticed that it was common to talk about birth as if it was something in the past. In contrast, adoption was always held in the present tense. "Juanita was born," but "Janine is adopted." Even stranger is the logic behind that use of language. It seems to make adoption and birth mutually exclusive. It is almost as if adoptive children were never born.

Practical

Adoptive families have the right to claim the language of adoption. The words we choose and those we use with our children will set the tone for those around us. How we talk about adoption—and whether we do—communicates more to our children than it does to others who may be listening. Positive and affirming language can help our kids feel more secure in who they are and how they came to us.

Further, it is possible to gently correct those who, mostly unintentionally, use terms that may make an adoptive child feel less a part of his family than other children. As parents, we are responsible for educating people who have an ongoing presence in our children's lives. The words we've chosen to use should be shared with all our close friends and relatives. Universal language crusades, however, are neither necessary nor productive.

As children become ready to attend school, a whole new set of challenges arises. Classroom projects, especially those in the early grades, can present unforeseen difficulties for adoptive children. Some of our kids simply don't have baby photos that they can share with their classmates. Others, like our daughter, will never know what they weighed at birth. The concept of a "family tree" is far too narrow for children who enjoy relationships with both birth and adoptive family members. A simple and direct conversation with your child's teacher as soon as such assignments are given almost always solves any problems your child might have. I've yet to encounter any teacher unwilling to help by being a bit creative when it mattered.

Words change our perceptions of ourselves and of others. The language we use to express our experience of reality shapes how we experience that reality. Without contradicting what is objectively true, in a certain sense, we are what we are said to be. The trick lies in knowing just who is doing the saying!

Think it through

⤜ What new words have you and your family learned from the experience of adopting a child?

⤜ Have you encountered a way of speaking about adoption that really bothers you?

⤜ How would you gently correct someone who uses words in a way that is negatively charged for your adoptive child?

⤜ How do you speak about adoption? Have you considered asking your friend or family member about how to use words in a more positive and affirming way?

Pray it through

HOLY SPIRIT, INSPIRATION OF THE WORD, give us the words we need to affirm our children. Help us to think and speak creatively, to find ways to express what you have done in our lives with gratitude and wonder. Keep us from words that hurt, that open up old wounds or threaten new injuries. Guide our interactions with others who are ignorant or insensitive. Show us how to share our lives with them in positive ways. Help us to speak love and commitment to one another and to bring that language of love to all we meet. Amen.

CHAPTER 37

Meeting Needs

Love Is Resourceful

I lift up my eyes to the hills—
from where will my help come?
My help comes from the Lord,
who made heaven and earth.

— Psalm 121:1–2

Reflection

God consoles us when we are overwhelmed and exhausted. The Holy Spirit is our Comforter, our help in times of distress. God does not help us from a distance. Our Father sends the Spirit to be with us and within us. That Spirit knows how hard we try, how bad we may feel, how hopeless things may look to us. God does not leave us, no matter what dark places of the soul our tears take us to. Gently, the Lifegiver brings us back. He guides us to the streams of divine presence. Allowing us to walk alongside the running waters, God sets our weary feet on a path straight and smooth, one on which we will not stumble.

All we need to do is lift up our eyes. God will take care of lifting our hearts. If we come to our Father, we will find the rest we need and the comfort we desire. God's love does not change because of our shortcomings. Instead, the Lord reveals the depths of his love for us. There is no fault or inadequacy that God cannot help us to overcome. There is no reason for sadness, but if we feel sad anyway, God reaches out with the consolation and help only the Holy One can give.

PERSONAL

I had some pretty unrealistic expectations of myself in parenting our adopted daughter. Raising so many children, I doubted that I would be thrown any pitches I had never seen before. Even if I couldn't hit them out of the park, I felt certain that I would manage to get on base.

Yulia, however, was an entirely different ball game, so to speak. Although she wasn't much different from what I expected her to be, my skills in handling her most definitely were. After seven children, I felt a crisis of confidence. I did a lot of second-guessing my responses to her, and I felt as if I was striking out with her on a daily basis. There didn't appear to be any home field advantage. It didn't help that I was, without a doubt, my own worst umpire.

There were days I wondered if adopting any child had been a very big mistake. It wasn't that I didn't love Yulia. Much to the contrary, my doubts surfaced because I loved her. I knew that Yulia was worth the work. It's just that I felt unequal to what she needed. There was no turning back. The choices had already been made, and I had to find a way to live with them.

At the end of a particularly difficult day, I realized I didn't really have a problem with what our lives were actually like. Objectively, everything was going well. My discontent was rooted in the disjuncture between reality and my expectations. Living wasn't the issue; living up to expectations was. I felt exhausted, inadequate, and just plain down. I decided to let things go and stop being so hard on myself. Within a few weeks, Yulia adjusted markedly, and my batting average improved.

PRACTICAL

Parents who feel sad and overwhelmed may find consolation in knowing that they are by no means alone. Though we may expect to be walking on air, negative emotions shouldn't come as a surprise to us. Completing an adoption is not unlike getting married, buying a house, or caring for someone who is sick. Suddenly, the whirlwind stops. There is an unavoidable emotional let down after the flurry of the adoption process is over.

When a child comes home, the "goal" is accomplished and the real work of parenting begins. That work can be rather mundane, repetitive, even boring. It can also be unrelenting, frustrating, or overwhelming. Whatever the case, parenting is the most demanding job on earth. Adoptive children are often especially needy, leaving parents with more of their own needs unmet.

New parents, who may have unwittingly romanticized family life, may not feel as fulfilled as they had hoped. Unfortunately, waiting patiently to have a child doesn't make raising one any easier. Constructing those idyllic Norman Rockwell-esque scenes we all imagine takes longer than we anticipated. Breaking them down, however, can be done in a matter of minutes, and finding out that they were merely paintings on a canvas, seconds. Suddenly, we find ourselves back at the easel with little motivation to paint much of anything at all.

Post-Adoptive Depression Syndrome (PADS) is very real. It is also relatively common. If you experience depression-like symptoms, you may profit from addressing your situation with a health professional. PADS does not mean that you love your children any less. Nor does PADS indicate that you are a bad or less-than-adequate parent. What it might mean is that you need to take the bull a bit less by the horns and allow yourself more time to adjust to your new family responsibilities. Forget about the housekeeping and haute cuisine for a while. No one ever died from a few weeks with dust bunnies or frozen dinners!

Think it through

- ⚜ Are your expectations of yourself unreasonable or harsh in any way?

- ⚜ Is there something you can "let go" of for a while to reduce stress in your family?

- ⚜ Who can you go to for comfort when you feel inadequate?

- ⚜ Is there something you can do to comfort your friends or family members when things don't go according to expectations?

Pray it through

HOLY SPIRIT, SOURCE OF HEAVENLY WATER, overflow our souls. Protect us from discouragement and exhaustion. Fill us with hope when we are tempted to despair. Reassure us when we doubt. Guide our expectations and keep us from being too hard on others or on ourselves. Strengthen us when we are overwhelmed. Be with us in the midst of our struggles. In meeting the needs of our children, show us how to have our needs met as well. Set our feet on a smooth path and lift us when we stumble. Lead us and our children to the cool streams of your presence, and give us the consolation we need to go on. Amen.

CHAPTER 38

Making You Mine

Love Never Fails

I am my beloved's and my beloved is mine . . .

— SONG OF SOLOMON 6:3

Love never ends.

— 1 CORINTHIANS 13:8

REFLECTION

Each one of us is the beloved of God. Many, however, do not feel the reality of the Father's love. Perhaps like the beloved in the Song of Solomon, we are afraid or unnerved. Perhaps it is because we want to be the one to take the initiative. Whatever the reason, the end result is the same. We do not feel that we belong to God or that he belongs to us. In wanting the Lover to belong to us, we do not see ourselves as "beloved." We overlook the sweetness of belonging to him.

Belonging is mutual, not individual. People become ours when we become theirs. The same holds true in our lives of faith. After all, the spiritual life is meant to be a love song. Our Father desires for us to belong to him and to one another. God is always seeking to make us his own. Taking us into his heart, the Holy Spirit waits for us to invite him into ours. The Lord so loves us that he gives himself completely into our hands. God does not make us his, that is, he does not force us to belong to him. Instead, the divine Lover makes himself ours. The Eternal One gifts himself to us with a love that never fails and does not end.

Personal

About nine months after she first came home, Yulia took command of the dinner table conversation. Waiting until everyone was listening, she began to make an announcement. "My name is Ju-li-a-na Chris-tine Wolfe." Smiling at how cute she was, we all started to pick up where we had left off. Yulia, however, wasn't finished. She continued, "Call me Juliana. I'm not Yulia or Yulka or any of those other names." My eyes filled up with tears. I asked her if that was what she really wanted. "Juliana," she said, and with that, Yulia disappeared.

I have always thought of that November supper as the day our daughter adopted us. No judge was present, no papers were necessary, and no translators were needed. Juliana had left her old life behind. She was ready—at that moment—to define herself in a new way, by a name that we had given her. Our daughter was truly ours not because we had a piece of paper that said she was, but because she had said so herself.

Up until that time, all the decisions that affected Juliana's life had been made by other people: her birth mother, government officials, an orphanage director, and us. When a judge in a Russian court concurred, she got onto a plane with us and flew halfway around the world. But on that November evening, Juliana articulated that something had changed, and what she felt counted in ways it had never counted before. Juliana had become part of something greater than herself. She was part of a family; she was ours and we were hers.

Recently, as I helped Juliana prepare for high school, I realized just how far she has come. The distance our daughter has traveled is much greater than the number of miles from Russia to the United States, and substantially more than eight time zones. Not as afraid as she used to be, Juliana doesn't move, or speak, or cry, or even eat the way she did when she first came to us. She is not the little orphan girl we met in Voronezh.

PRACTICAL

Adoption is not a court date. It is a lifelong practice of loving. The adoption process never ends, and even a dozen years after we bring our children home, it is not yet truly complete. As we live more of our lives together as family, we continue to find new gaps to bridge and new ways of belonging to each other.

When we adopt, we make a gift of our hearts and lives to a child. We do not know whether our sons and daughters will ever give themselves to us. Yet, like the Spirit who inspires us, we do it just the same. We choose to belong to our children in the hope that our children will someday belong to us.

Family is a journey that never ends, one that has always only just begun. No matter how long or far we have traveled together, there is so much more ahead for us to become to each other. As our children grow into adolescence and adulthood, our paths invariably twist and turn. There are days when light is dim, and nights that make us question whether morning will ever come. But, through every darkness we encounter, the light of hope shines in our homes. Like the North Star, our places are fixed in one another's hearts.

God's love teaches us to give what we have received. Through living by faith every day, we belong more to God and become more like him. The purpose of our lives is to become God's completely. Knowing the Father's love for us the way our children know our love for them, we pass from belonging to belonging. At the end of our journey, when all is still, we will listen to the voices of those at heaven's table pronouncing the names by which they will be called. And as eternal day is dawning, we will hear the song of songs rise from the home that the Holy Spirit has made in our hearts. "I am my Beloved's," we will sing, and the Lord will answer, "My beloved is mine!"

Think it through

- Are there things that make you feel like you belong to someone? What are they?

- Do you see your child's adoption as a gift he or she receives, or as a gift your child can also give?

- How far has your family come? What joys do you look forward to in the years ahead?

- Is there something you can do to express how grateful you are to have your family members or friends and their children be part of your life?

Pray it through

HOLY SPIRIT, SPIRIT OF ADOPTION, continue to lead us, not only in what we do, but in how we think, in how we decide, in how we see ourselves and others. Bring us to the love that makes us truly yours. Help us to bear that same love to our children. May your fruit in our lives—love, joy, peace, patience, kindness, generosity, faithfulness, gentleness, and self-control—sustain our lives together. May your presence with us sweeten our days and fill our hearts. Teach us to give ourselves as you do: freely and totally as gift. Give us the grace to accept the gift of self that others—even our children—long to give us. Help us to hear your call throughout our lives and to answer it according to your will. Amen.

Order for the Blessing of Parents and an Adopted Child

Introduction

302 The adoption of a child is an important event in the lives of a married couple or a single parent. This blessing serves as a public thanksgiving for the precious gift of a child and as a welcome of the child into its new family.

303 If the child is old enough to respond, provision is made for the child to accept the new parents as his or her own. In this case, the introduction of the rite should be adapted to the circumstances, and a more appropriate reading may be chosen.

304 If there is only one parent, the rite should be adapted to the circumstances by the minister.

305 This order may be used by a priest or a deacon, and also by a layperson, who follows the rites and prayers designated for a lay minister.

Order of Blessing

Introductory Rites

306 When the community has gathered, a suitable song may be sung. After the singing, the minister says:

> **In the name of the Father, and of the Son, and of the Holy Spirit.**

All make the sign of the cross and reply:

> **Amen.**

307 A minister who is a priest or deacon greets those present in the following or other suitable words, taken mainly from sacred Scripture.

> **May the love of God be with you always.**

And all reply:

> **And with your spirit.**

308 A lay minister greets those present in the following words:

> **Let us praise our loving God.**
> **Blessed be God for ever.**
>
> **R. Blessed be God for ever.**

309 In the following or similar words, the minister prepares those present for the blessing.

It has pleased God our heavenly Father to answer the earnest prayers of N. and N. for the gift of a child. Today we join them in offering heartfelt thanks for the joyful and solemn responsibility which becomes theirs by the arrival of N. into their family.

Reading of the Word of God

310 A reader, another person present, or the minister reads a text of sacred Scripture.

Brothers and sisters, listen to the words of the holy gospel according to Mark 10:13–16:

Jesus blesses the little children.

People were bringing children to Jesus that he might touch them, but the disciples rebuked the people. When Jesus saw this he became indignant and said to the disciples, "Let the children come to me; do not prevent them, for the kingdom of God belongs to such as these. Amen, I say to you, whoever does not accept the kingdom of God like a child will not enter it." Then he embraced the children and blessed them, placing his hands on them.

311 Or:

(Descriptions following Scripture references below added by the author.)

- **Deuteronomy 6:4–7:** The Great Commandment. You shall love the Lord God with all your heart, with all your soul, and with all your strength.

- **Deuteronomy 31:12–13:** The Reading of the Law. Gather men, women, and children so they may hear God's law and learn to fear the Lord.

- **1 Samuel 1:9–11, 20–28; 2:26:** Hannah Keeps Her Word. For this child I prayed . . . now I, in turn, give him to the Lord.

- **Matthew 18:1–4:** Jesus Speaks to His Disciples. Whoever humbles himself like a child is the greatest in heaven.

Luke 2:22–32, 52: The Presentation of Jesus in the Temple. My eyes have seen your salvation.

312 As circumstances suggest, one of the following responsorial psalms may be sung, or some other suitable song.

R. O Lord, our God, how wonderful your name in all the earth!

PSALM 8

O Lord, our Lord,
how glorious is your name over all the earth!
You have exalted your majesty above the heavens.
Out of the mouths of babes and sucklings
you have fashioned praise because of your foes,
to silence the hostile and the vengeful. **R.**

When I behold your heavens, the work of your fingers,
the moon and the stars which you set in place—
What is man that you should be mindful of him,
or the son of man that you should care for him? **R.**

You have made him little less than the angels,
and crowned him with glory and honor.
You have given him rule over the works of your hands,
putting all things under his feet: **R.**

All sheep and oxen,
yes, and the beasts of the field,
The birds of the air, the fishes of the sea,
and whatever swims the paths of the seas. **R.**

O Lord, our Lord,
how glorious is your name over all the earth! **R.**

Psalm 78:1–7

> **R. (v. 4) Tell the coming generations the glorious deeds**
>   **of the Lord.**

313 As circumstances suggest, the minister may give those present a brief explanation of the biblical text, so that they may understand through faith the meaning of the celebration.

Acknowledgment by the Child and Parents

314 The minister asks the parents:

> **You have received N. into your family;**
> **will you (continue to) love and care for him/her?**

Parents:

> **We will.**

315 If the child is old enough to answer, the minister asks:

> **You have accepted N. and N. as your parents;**
> **will you love and respect them?**

The child replies:

> **I will.**

316 The minister says:

> **As God has made us all his children by grace and adoption,**
> **may this family always abide in his love.**

The Canticle of Mary or another hymn of praise may then be sung.

Intercessions

317 The intercessions are then said. The minister introduces them and an assisting minister or one of those present announces the intentions. From the following those best suited to the occasion may be used or adapted, or other intentions that apply to the particular circumstances may be composed.

The minister says:

> God is the author of all life and calls us into his loving family; with thankful hearts we pray:

> **R. Loving Father, hear us.**

Assisting minister:

> For the Church throughout the world, that it may nurture, guide, protect and love all who are joined to it in baptism, let us pray to the Lord. **R.**

Assisting minister:

> For N. and N. and their new son/daughter, N., that God may bind them together in love as a family in Christ, let us pray to the Lord. **R.**

Assisting minister:

> [For the brother(s) and sister(s) of N., that they may grow in friendship and love, let us pray to the Lord. **R.**]

Assisting minister:

> For married couples who desire the gift of a child, that God may hear their prayers, let us pray to the Lord. **R.**

Assisting minister:

> For all Christian families, that the love of Christ may dwell in their homes, let us pray to the Lord. **R.**

318 After the intercessions the minister, in the following or similar words, invites all present to sing or say the Lord's Prayer.

As God's children by adoption, we pray:

All:

Our Father . . .

Prayer of Blessing

319 A minister who is a priest or deacon says the prayer of blessing with hands outstretched over the parents and child; a lay minister says the prayer with hands joined.

Loving God,
your Son has taught us
that whoever welcomes a child in his name, welcomes him.
We give you thanks for N.,
whom N. and N. have welcomed into their family.
Bless this family.
Confirm a lively sense of your presence with them
and grant to these parents patience and wisdom,
that their lives may show forth the love of Christ
as they bring N. up to love all that is good.
We ask this through Christ our Lord.
R. Amen.

As circumstances suggest, the minister in silence may sprinkle the family with holy water.

Concluding Rite

320 A minister who is a priest or deacon concludes the rite by saying:

May almighty God, who has called us into the family of
Christ,

fill you with grace and peace,
now and for ever.

R. Amen.

Then he blesses all present.

And may almighty God bless you all,
the Father, and the Son, ✝ and the Holy Spirit.

R. Amen.

321 A lay minister concludes the rite by signing himself or herself
with the sign of the cross and saying:

May almighty God, who has called us into the family of
Christ, fill us with grace and peace, now and for ever.

R. Amen.

322 It is preferable to end the celebration with a suitable song.

ABOUT THE AUTHOR

 A wife and mother of eight, Jaymie Stuart Wolfe is an editor of children's and teen books at Pauline Books & Media. Jaymie's biweekly column has appeared in Boston's archdiocesan newspaper, *The Pilot*, since 1995. She converted to the Catholic faith in 1983 and has directed adult faith formation, children's sacramental preparation, and liturgical music ministry. She frequently speaks on living the faith and family life. Jaymie is a graduate of Harvard University and holds a master of arts in ministry degree from St. John's Seminary, Boston.

BOOKS & MEDIA

The Daughters of St. Paul operate book and media centers at the following addresses. Visit, call, or write the one nearest you today, or find us at www.pauline.org.

CALIFORNIA

3908 Sepulveda Blvd, Culver City, CA 90230	310-397-8676
935 Brewster Avenue, Redwood City, CA 94063	650-369-4230
5945 Balboa Avenue, San Diego, CA 92111	858-565-9181

FLORIDA

145 S.W. 107th Avenue, Miami, FL 33174	305-559-6715

HAWAII

1143 Bishop Street, Honolulu, HI 96813	808-521-2731

ILLINOIS

172 North Michigan Avenue, Chicago, IL 60601	312-346-4228

LOUISIANA

4403 Veterans Memorial Blvd, Metairie, LA 70006	504-887-7631

MASSACHUSETTS

885 Providence Hwy, Dedham, MA 02026	781-326-5385

MISSOURI

9804 Watson Road, St. Louis, MO 63126	314-965-3512

NEW YORK

64 W. 38th Street, New York, NY 10018	212-754-1110

SOUTH CAROLINA

243 King Street, Charleston, SC 29401	843-577-0175

TEXAS

Currently no book center; for parish exhibits or outreach evangelization, contact: 210-569-0500, or SanAntonio@paulinemedia.com, or P.O. Box 761416, San Antonio, TX 78245

VIRGINIA

1025 King Street, Alexandria, VA 22314	703-549-3806

CANADA

3022 Dufferin Street, Toronto, ON M6B 3T5	416-781-9131

¡También somos su fuente para libros,
videos y música en español!